W9-AQW-670

THE WORLD OF SCIENCE

GREAT DISCOVERIES AND INVENTIONS

DAVID LAMBERT & JANE INSLEY

Facts On File Publications
New York, New York • Bicester, England

GREAT DISCOVERIES AND INVENTIONS

First published in the United States of America in 1985 by Facts on File, Inc., 460 Park Avenue South, New York, N.Y.10016

First published in Great Britain in 1985 by Orbis Publishing Limited, London

Library of Congress Cataloging in Publication Data

Main entry under title:

World of Science

Includes index.
Summary: A twenty-five volume encyclopedia of scientific subjects, designed for eight- to twelve-year-olds. One volume is entirely devoted to projects.
Science—Dictionaries, Juvenile. Science—Dictionaries
Q121.J86 1984 500 84-1654

ISBN: 0-8160-1062-5

Printed in Yugoslavia
10 9 8 7 6 5 4 3 2

Consultant editors
Eleanor Felder, former managing editor, *Scientific American*
James Neujahr, Dean of the School of Education, City College of New York
Ethan Signer, Professor of Biology, Massachusetts Institute of Technology
J. Tuzo Wilson, Director General, Ontario Science Centre

Previous pages A ruby laser being used to create a hologram.

Editor Penny Clarke
Designer Roger Kohn

CONTENTS

1 THE DEVELOPMENT OF TECHNOLOGY

2 MAKING MATTER WORK FOR US

3 HARNESSING ENERGY

► A Thor Delta booster rocket is launched into space. Kerosene mixed with liquid oxygen provides the power for lift-off. Extra power for the launch comes from three small rockets that drop off when their fuel is used up.

Note There are some unusual words in this book. They are explained in the Glossary on pages 62–63. The first time a word is used in the text it is printed in *italics*.

1 THE DEVELOPMENT OF TECHNOLOGY

▼ Four finely made stone spear points. The flange opposite the point fitted into a socket in the wooden shaft and was held tightly in place with strips of leather.

THE FIRST DISCOVERIES

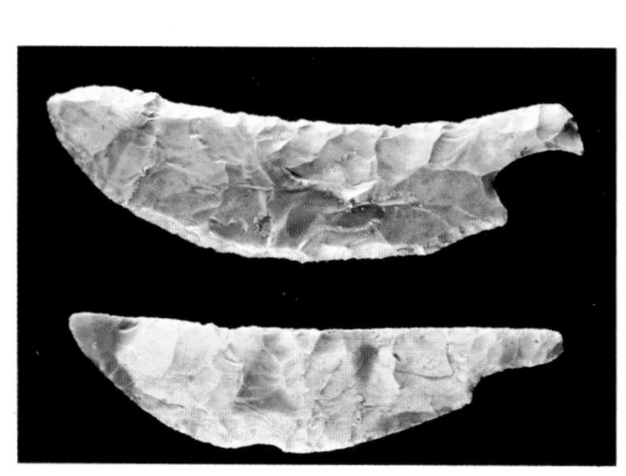

▲ **Above** The flanges of these two stone knife blades fitted into wooden handles in the same way as the spear points (**far right**). **Above right** These two stone axes are not as well made as the blades or the spear points – the edges do not look as sharp and very little of the rough surface of the original stone has been removed.

Imagine being washed up on a desert island with no clothes or tools. How would you find food, shelter, warmth and safety from wild beasts? Just staying alive would take up all your time.

Life was rather like this for early humans. Because life was so hard, people looked for ways to make it easier. For instance, over two million years ago they had discovered that it was easier to cut and scrape skins with sharp pebbles than with round ones. They had also learnt to chip away the surface of a pebble to make it sharp if there were no suitable ones around. By 25,000 years ago, Stone Age peoples were still discovering new and better ways of shaping stone tools to make them more efficient.

Stone tools were the first of thousands of discoveries and inventions. Bit by bit these helped mankind to change the surface of the earth in ways that have made people the masters of all other living things.

This first chapter of our book describes some of the most important discoveries and inventions through the ages.

Stone and fire

Some of the greatest discoveries were made by Stone Age peoples living long ago. Our early ancestors learnt to trim flakes of stone into the shapes of knives, spear blades, arrow-heads and scrapers. Large, sharp-pointed spears helped hunters to kill creatures larger and stronger than themselves. With arrows they could kill prey from a distance. Nimble-fingered women used bone needles and sinew 'threads' to sew animal skins together to make clothes that kept out the cold.

Meanwhile people had already learnt to keep alight fires started by a flash of lightning. Half a million years ago fires kept cave homes warm and bright at night, and scared off dangerous animal. Later, hunters learnt to set fire to areas of forest. Grass grew from the burnt ground. Large grass-eating animals, such as antelopes, moved in to graze. Then hunters killed and ate these grazers.

Speech

The discovery of speech had helped make

big-game hunting possible. Once people could explain ideas to each other, hunters could plan to work together to attack whole herds of horses or mammoths. With speech, old and experienced men and women could tell their children what they themselves had learnt. So discoveries and inventions lived on after the people who had made them died. Speech also helped new, useful ways of living spread around the world.

Farming and herding

New tools and know-how made people's lives less harsh and dangerous than they had been at first. But even 10,000 years ago most Stone Age people still had to hunt wild beasts or gather wild plants for their food. When these grew scarce many people starved. Meanwhile, though, in Asia, people were learning how to sow and reap food plants. These were mostly wild grasses and were developed into today's wheat and barley. These people were among the world's first farmers. Soon, too, some hunters learnt to catch and tame wild sheep and cattle. These early herdsmen and shepherds began keeping creatures for meat, milk and wool.

Farming and herding produced a surer food supply than hunting and gathering had done. So fewer people starved and mankind multiplied.

▲ A very ancient painting found on a rock in the Sahara. It shows a group of prehistoric hunters chasing wild animals.

▲ These paintings from an ancient Egyptian tomb show how farming had developed in the Middle East about 4000 years ago:**Top** a farmer harvests his corn with a sickle and **below**, cultivated date palms bear a good crop of fruit.

▲ The first towns and cities developed in fertile areas where the farmers could provide food for many people. Towns and cities attracted trade and wealth and soon fine temples and palaces were built – these are the ruins of the observatory at Macchu Picchu, the ancient Inca City in Peru. Buildings such as this are also the sign of a settled community – a community at war needs soldiers, not builders.

Farming led to the development of cities. It came about like this. Early farmers settled down in villages to tend their crops. In the Middle East, some villagers learnt new and better ways of growing crops on rich river-valley soils. They dug ditches to bring water to their plots of land. They harnessed oxen to ploughs. With an ox's muscle power, each farmer could cultivate more land than he could dig by hand. So he produced more than enough food for his family.

Farmers began exchanging spare food for useful tools made by skilful craftsmen, so these people no longer needed to produce food for themselves. They worked full-time at making things such as metal tools, clay storage pots, or woven clothes and carpets.

A rich area of farmland could feed many specialists like these. Instead of working on the land, and living in small, scattered villages, they lived in towns. By 5,000 years ago some towns had grown into cities, where kings and priests raised splendid tombs and temples.

Making tools from metal

It was trade that kept each city going. This trade depended heavily on metalsmiths who made the blades of tools and weapons wanted by farmers and soldiers. No one knows how metal-working started. But by 8,000 years ago someone in the Middle East had found that if certain rocks were made extremely hot, melted *copper* came out of them. Craftsmen learnt to pour this molten copper into moulds shaped as a knife blade or an axehead. As the copper cooled, it hardened in that useful shape. People quickly discovered that metal tools could be as hard and strong as stone, but did not break so easily.

◀ As trade between communities developed, various systems of money and coins developed – it is really very difficult to buy and sell on a large scale without money.

◀ A carving of a wheeled vehicle used in the Middle East about 4000 years ago. The invention of the wheel also helped trade because a cart could carry far more goods than a person or a pack-animal.

Trade and transport

Trade in food and metal tools sparked off many inventions and discoveries that made it possible to live in cities. Among the most important developments were weights, money, mathematics and writing. Weights helped merchants measure what they sold. Money made it possible to buy and sell all kinds of things, instead of swapping just a few. Mathematics helped them do the necessary sums. Writing helped them keep a record of these transactions.

The growing need for trade encouraged inventions that made it easier to shift large loads long distances by land or sea. Wheeled carts could carry more than men or animals could carry on their backs. Wind-driven sailing ships became large and strong enough to sail the open sea.

These are just a few of the important technological inventions that had been made by 2,000 years ago.

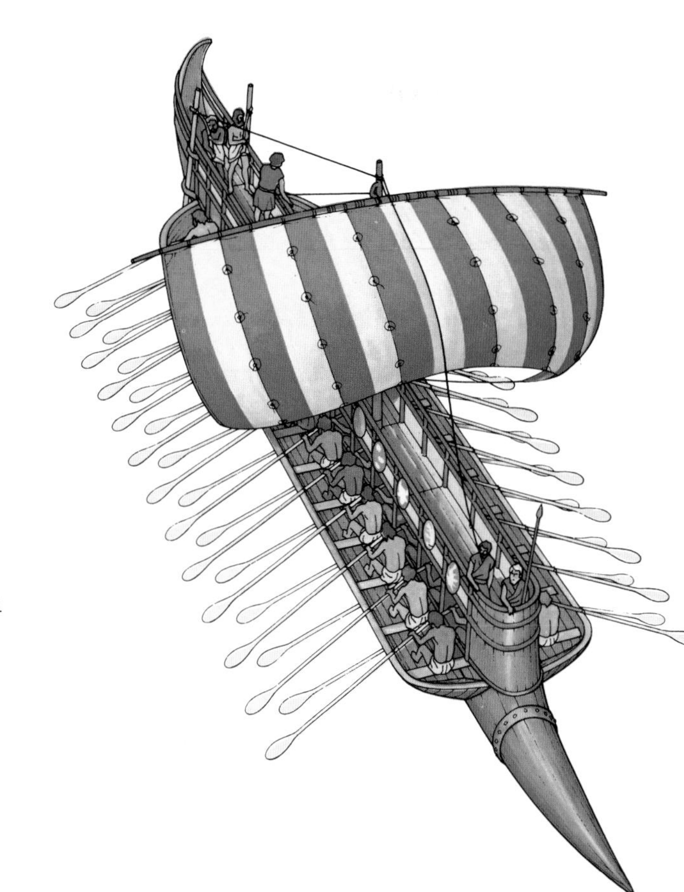

◀ This is a reconstruction of a Phoenician war galley – the pointed bow was designed to ram and hole enemy ships. Similar galleys, rowed by slaves but without the pointed bow, were used to carry goods along the coast of the Mediterranean.

THE AGE OF INVENTIONS

► The new calendar introduced by the revolutionary government of France during the French Revolution (1789–99).

▲ Johann Gutenberg invented printing around 1436. This page is from a Bible he printed probably in 1452.

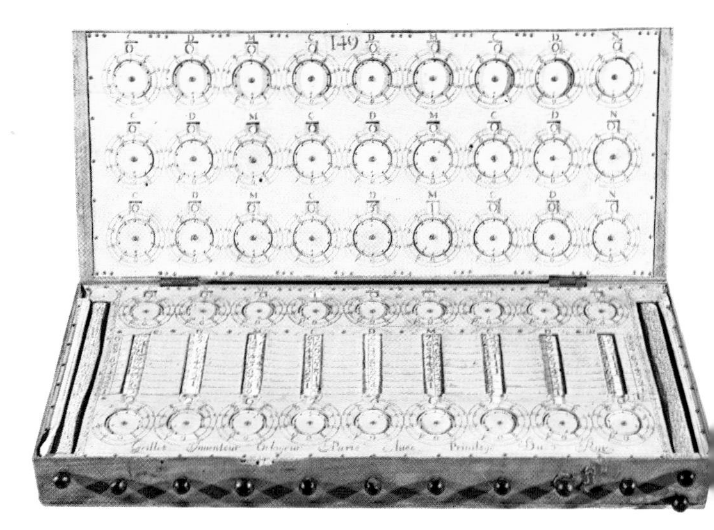

▼ Blaise Pascal, the French scientist and mathematician who lived from 1623–62, designed this adding machine. Although very crude, in many ways it is the ancestor of today's pocket calculators.

Our modern age of discovery and invention began in the fifteenth century AD. In that century, new navigation instruments and types of ship helped sailors to discover unknown continents. The first printed books appeared. Clockmakers built accurate time-keeping mechanisms. These inventions were the work of craftsmen.

Scientific discovery

Scientific discovery began with the Italian Galileo Galilei (1564–1642). Galileo developed the scientific way of solving problems: you suggest an answer, then plan and carry out experiments to find out if your suggestion is right. This is known as the scientific method and is still used today.

By the early 1600s, scientists were using new instruments such as thermometers, barometers, microscopes and telescopes. These helped them study things around them, from the inside of the human body to the far-off stars and planets.

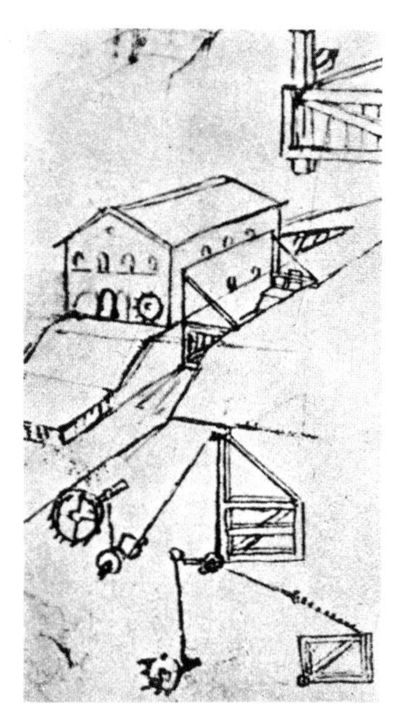

▲ A page from one of Leonardo da Vinci's sketchbooks. He was a great inventor as well as an artist. He died in 1519.

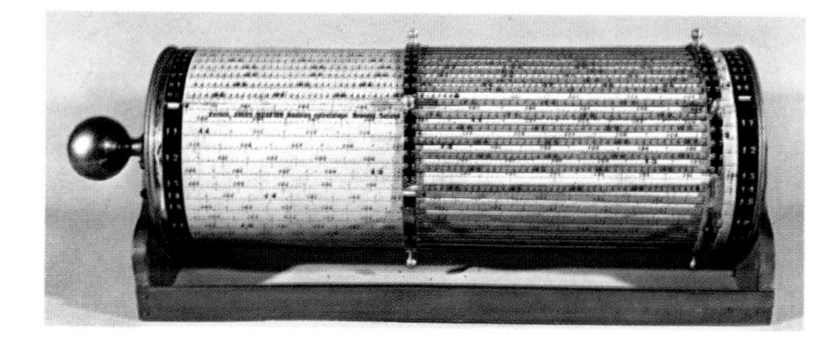

◄ A machine made in the 19th century to help mathematicians calculate complicated logarithms.

▲ A small portable sundial made in Germany in the 17th century. Shadows cast by the metal 'fins' showed the time.

▶ The great Italian scientist Galileo Galilei (1564–1642) developed a microscope. He arranged glass lenses in a tube so that they would magnify objects placed under the microscope.

◀ This odd-looking object is a thermometer made in Italy in the 17th century. Many great discoveries and inventions were made during the Renaissance, the great period of scientific and artistic achievement that began in Italy in the 14th century and gradually spread to the rest of Europe.

Machines and mass-production
It was the inventions of craftsmen, not scientists, that started changing people's lives, in the 1700s and 1800s. The chief inventions were *machines* built of *iron* and powered by steam produced by burning coal. Machines began cheaply mass producing clothes and other goods in city factories. By 1900 machines were helping farmers to produce more food than ever. And canning and refrigeration provided new ways of storing food.

Big steam-powered ships and trains began taking huge amounts of goods made in North America and Europe to countries all around the world. The ships and trains brought back food from vast new farms opened up in far-off lands such as Argentina and Australia.

◀ Making iron in France in 1850. Earlier improvements in the refining process helped make the industrial boom of the 19th century possible.

◀ A 19th-century steam plough in operation. A steam engine was placed at each end of a field and the plough was pulled backwards and forwards across the field between them.

How invention shapes our lives
In this century, scientists have added greatly to discoveries about the way that everything is made and works. Now, too, teams of scientists and other experts share their knowledge to help make fresh inventions. Thanks to their efforts, machines now perform much of the hard work once carried out by human muscles. Machines help to make most of us much better fed and better off than were our ancestors a century ago. Invention and discovery mean, too, that the world can feed more people than ever before.

The next two chapters of this book pick out some of the most important and intriguing inventions and discoveries that help, or could help, shape our lives.

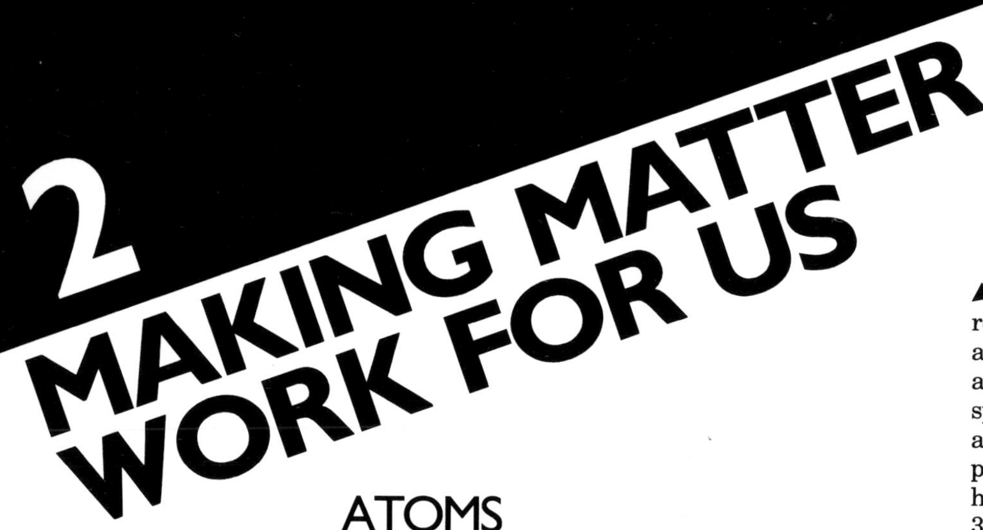

2 MAKING MATTER WORK FOR US

ATOMS

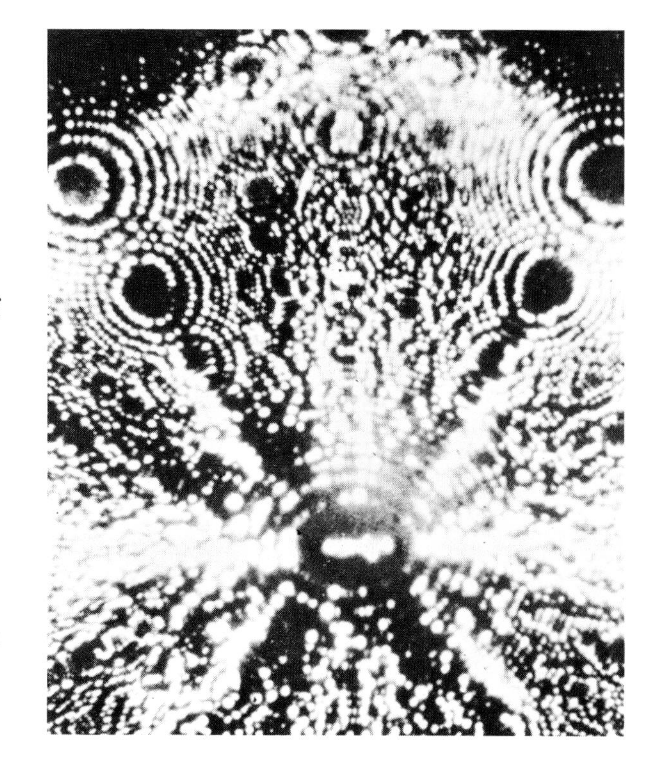

▲ A photograph revealing the atoms in a needle-tip. Each atom shows up as a spot of light. Groups of atoms form a crystal pattern. This pattern has been magnified 3 million times.

▲ In 400 BC Democritus thought atoms were made up of the same material but had different shapes.

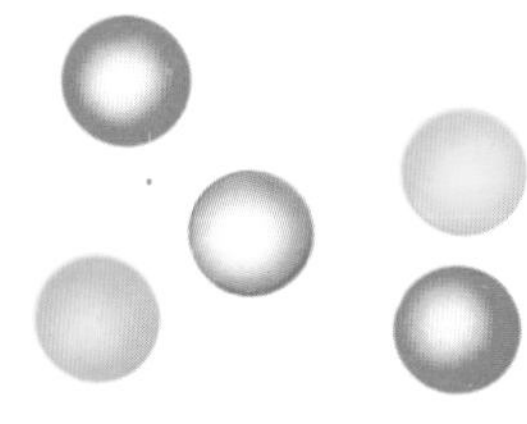

▲ In 1803 John Dalton suggested there were a few kinds of atoms, each kind made of different material.

▲ In 1897 Joseph Thomson discovered that the electrons in an atom were surrounded by a cloud of positive electrical charges.

▲ By 1911 Ernest Rutherford had shown that an atom's electrons move around a heavy nucleus with a positive electric charge.

All matter – every substance you can think of – is made of tiny particles called *atoms*. Your body is made up of billions upon billions of atoms. Billions more make up your home, the soil and rock beneath it, the air above.

Iron and more than 90 other substances each consist of atoms of one kind. We call these substances *elements*. But many substances contain two or more kinds of atom, closely bound together. Such substances are compounds. For example, water is a *compound* made of oxygen atoms and *hydrogen* atoms. Each smallest particle (or *molecule*) of water is made of two hydrogen atoms joined to one oxygen atom.

Particles too small to be cut

The idea of the atom is extremely old. It started with Democritus, an ancient Greek philosopher. About 400 BC Democritus suggested that if you cut anything in half, then halved each half, and so on, you would end up with a particle too small to be divided yet again. Democritus called this particle *atomos*, a Greek word for 'uncuttable'. Democritus believed that everything was made of atoms. He even thought that different substances were made of different kinds or mixtures of atoms. Other philosophers rejected such ideas. Now we know that Democritus came close to the truth.

The first truly modern ideas about atoms date from 1803. In that year, the English chemist John Dalton argued scientifically that all elements consist of atoms. He thought that in each element all atoms are identical. He even worked out that different kinds of atom differ in weight. For instance, iron atoms weigh more than hydrogen atoms, while oxygen atoms weigh more than those of hydrogen but less than those of iron. Dalton's work excited other chemists. They tried to work out exactly how the weights of different atoms compared, so that they could arrange the atoms and the elements in order. The first to group the elements this way was Dmitri Mendeleev, a Russian chemist, working in the 1860s.

Inside an atom

Until the 1890s scientists imagined atoms as tiny solid particles. Then in 1897 the English physicist, Joseph Thomson, discovered tiny particles with a negative *electric charge*. Each particle was only one-thousandth the weight of a hydrogen atom, the lightest kind of atom known. Scientists named these 'new' particles *electrons*.

So it seemed that atoms were not the smallest particles of all. Scientists began to think each atom must be rather like a raisin cake with electrons as the 'raisins'. They supposed the 'cake' itself had a positive electric charge that cancelled out the electrons' negative charge. That made sense, for positive and negative electric charges attract each other. Maybe, then, these charges held the ingredients of the 'cake' together.

In 1911 the British physicist Ernest Rutherford studied fresh experiments with tiny particles and came up with another explanation. Rutherford decided that each atom was mostly empty space. He thought that atoms had a solid nucleus or centre, with a positive charge. Around this lay empty space through which electrons whirled.

Since then, new finds have made our idea of the atom more complicated still. At first it seemed that the *atomic nucleus* was just made of positively charged particles, or *protons*. But, in 1932 James Chadwick found that the nucleus also had electrically neutral particles called *neutrons*. Since then, scientists using special instruments have tracked down many other particles inside the nuclei of atoms. They have found, too, how to split an atom – an achievement Democritus would have thought impossible.

◀ This is the modern picture of an atom. Electrons (black dots) move in orbits (loops) around the nucleus at set distances called shells (shown red, green and blue).

The inner shell can hold only 2 electrons, the next 8 and so on.

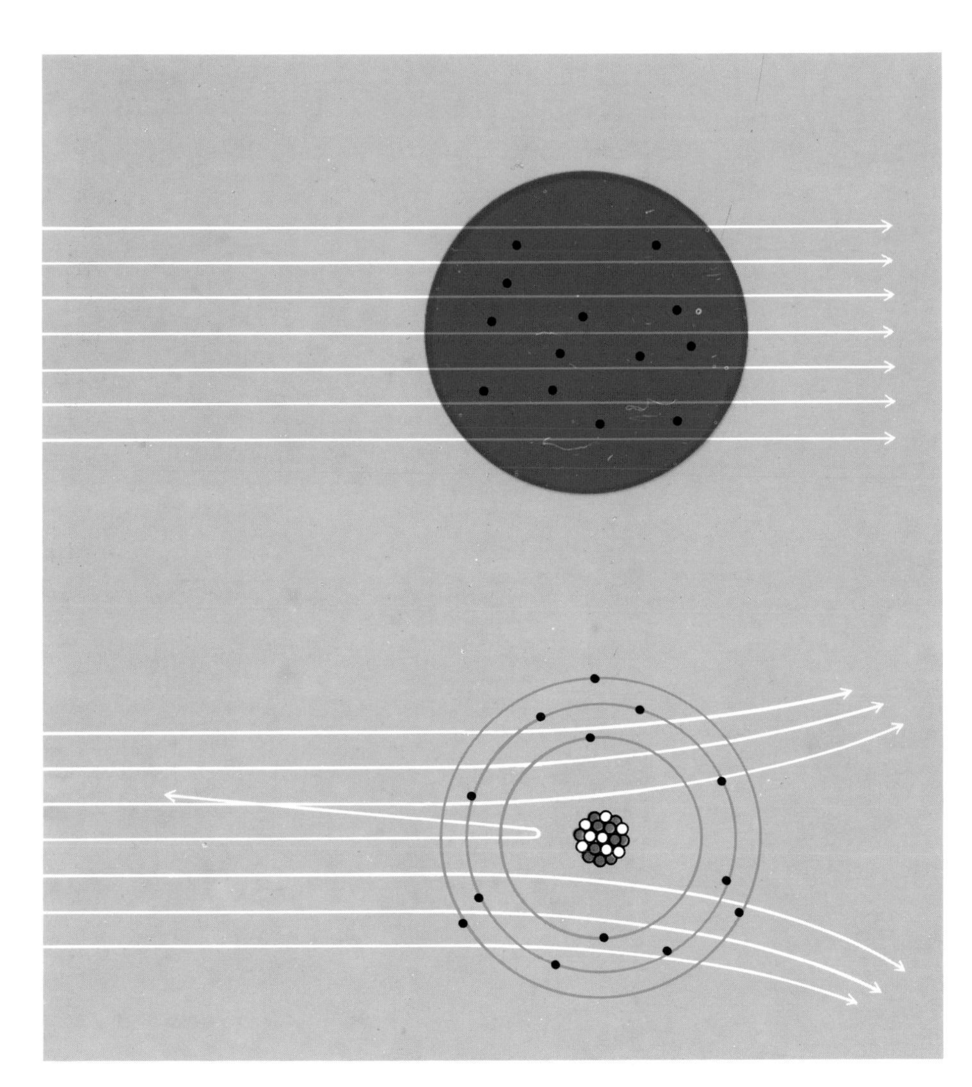

◀ This shows how Ernest Rutherford found that atoms had a 'core'. He fired so-called alpha particles at a metal sheet. If all particles went through (top) it meant that a positive electricial charge (red) was spread all through each atom. In fact some particles bounced back (bottom). This showed that they had hit tiny cores inside the atoms. Black dots shown here stand for electrons.

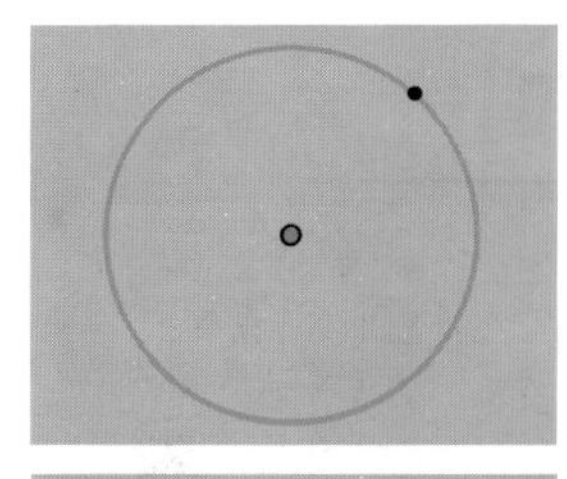

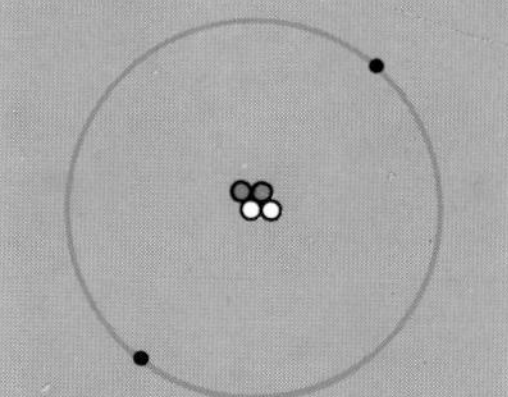

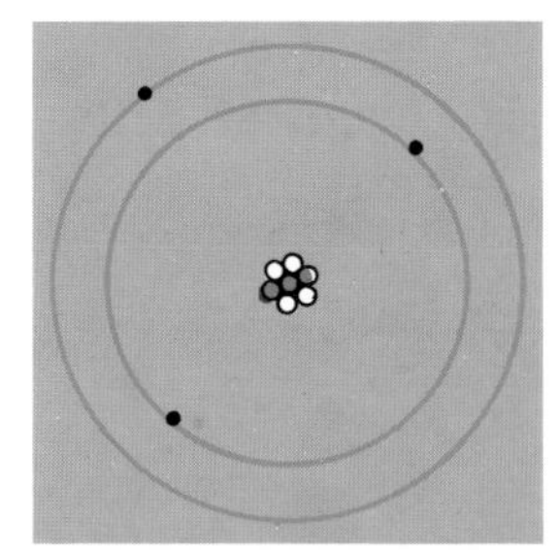

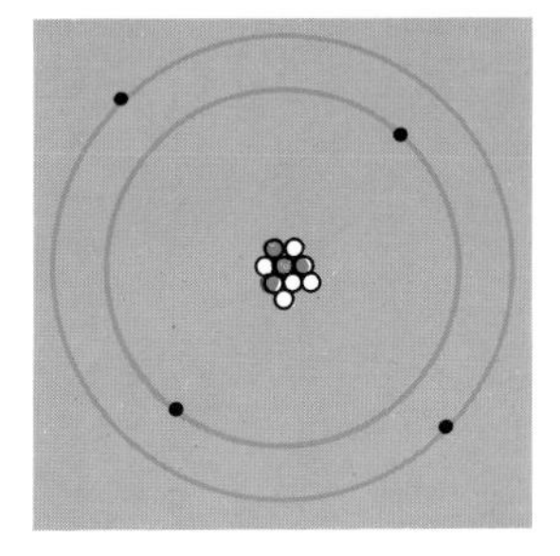

▶ Diagram showing the differences between the numbers of particles in the cores of four kinds of atom. Particles are protons (red) and neutrons (white). From top to bottom, are hydrogen, helium, lithium and beryllium. Black dots show electrons orbiting the cores – one electron for each proton.

MICROSCOPE

The human eye is one of nature's most wonderful creations. Yet your eyes cannot see objects less than a few thousandths of a centimetre across. This means that a whole world of bacteria and other very tiny things remains invisible to the unaided eye. But we can study and enjoy that world by looking at it through a microscope. This instrument takes its name from Greek words for 'small' and 'look'.

Early microscopes

The first microscopes were of the kind called light or optical microscopes because they use light to reveal objects. A light microscope may house one or more *lenses*. Lenses are pieces of curved glass that bend the light passing through them. The lenses in a microscope bend light passing through them from an object in such a way that you see a magnified image, or picture, of that object.

► Two diagrams compare a light microscope (**far right**) and an electron microscope (**right**). In the light microscope, light waves pass through the specimen to be magnified. Objective lenses bend light from the object to make an enlarged, upside-down image. A projector-lens system enlarges the image again, turns it right way up, and projects it to the observer's eye. An electron microscope can enlarge details smaller than the wave-length of visible light. A beam of electrons passes through the specimen and electric or magnetic fields serve as lenses to enlarge its image. This shows up on a special fluorescent screen.

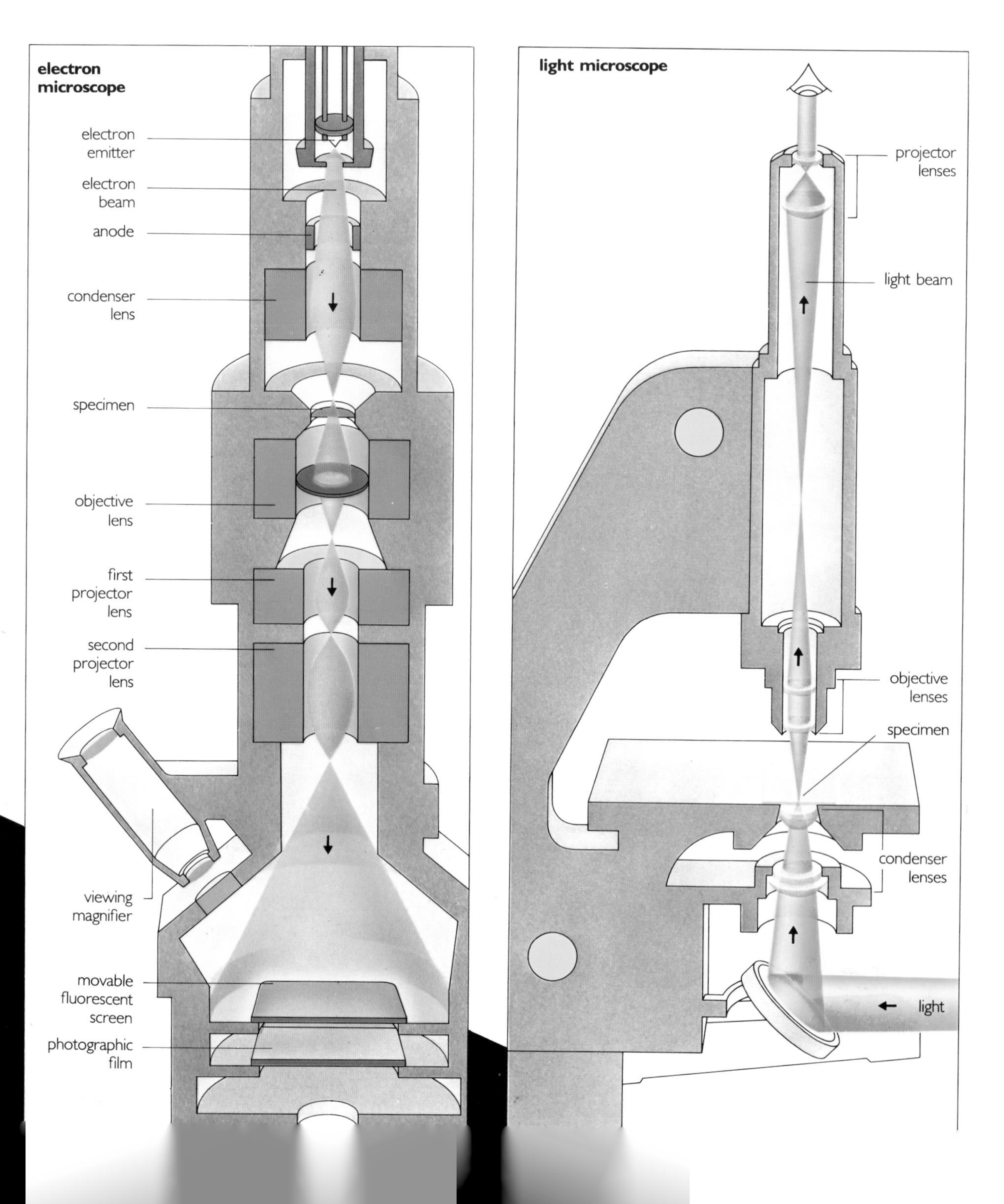

The simplest light microscopes have only one lens. At least 3,000 years ago the engravers who made beautifully carved but tiny seals and ornaments probably magnified their work by gazing at it through a glass globe filled with water. This acted as a crude lens. But glass lenses of a modern type appeared seven centuries ago when inventors first developed spectacles. In the 1660s a Dutch merchant named Anton van Leeuwenhoek made a simple microscope from just a single tiny lens. He ground this into shape so perfectly that it could magnify an object clearly by about 200 times.

Microscopes with several lenses can be more powerful than that. Back in 1590 the Dutch spectacle makers Hans and Zacharias Janssen had already made a two-lens microscope. The eye lens, placed near the eye, had an inward curving (concave) surface. The surface of the objective lens, placed near the object to be magnified, was convex (curving outward). Such early so-called compound microscopes gave distorted images. But by the 1660s, the English scientist Robert Hooke had a compound microscope good enough for him to discover and identify cells – the kinds of 'building block' that go to make all living matter. Some modern light microscopes with several lenses can magnify up to 2,500 times.

Magnifying a million times

New, immensely powerful kinds of microscope have appeared since 1930. One of these is the *electron microscope*. Instead of using glass lenses to bend light, this microscope uses electric and magnetic fields to bend beams of tiny particles called electrons. A magnetic lens focuses electrons on the object to be magnified. They pass right through it, but this scatters them. The scattered electrons pass through other lenses. Then they hit a kind of 'television' screen that glows where each electron makes a hit. The pattern on the screen is an image of the object, magnified. Scientists can view or photograph the screen, and the photographs can be enlarged. In this way electron microscopes can magnify the image of an object by one million times.

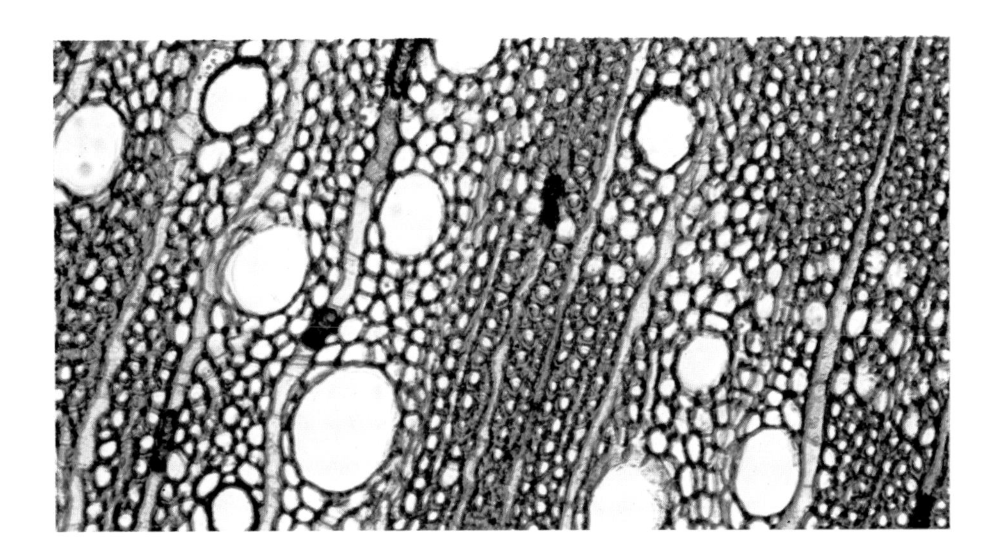

▲ Cells in oak wood look like this when stained and seen through a powerful microscope. Staining makes the cells show up clearly.

In 1958 the German physicist Erwin Müller invented the field ion microscope which showed how atoms are arranged inside a piece of metal. This microscope magnified up to three million times. Today, microscopes can magnify over seven million times.

Only scientists use powerful microscopes like these. But anyone can learn to have fun with a light microscope. Its lenses will show you that a drop of pond water is full of fascinating structures.

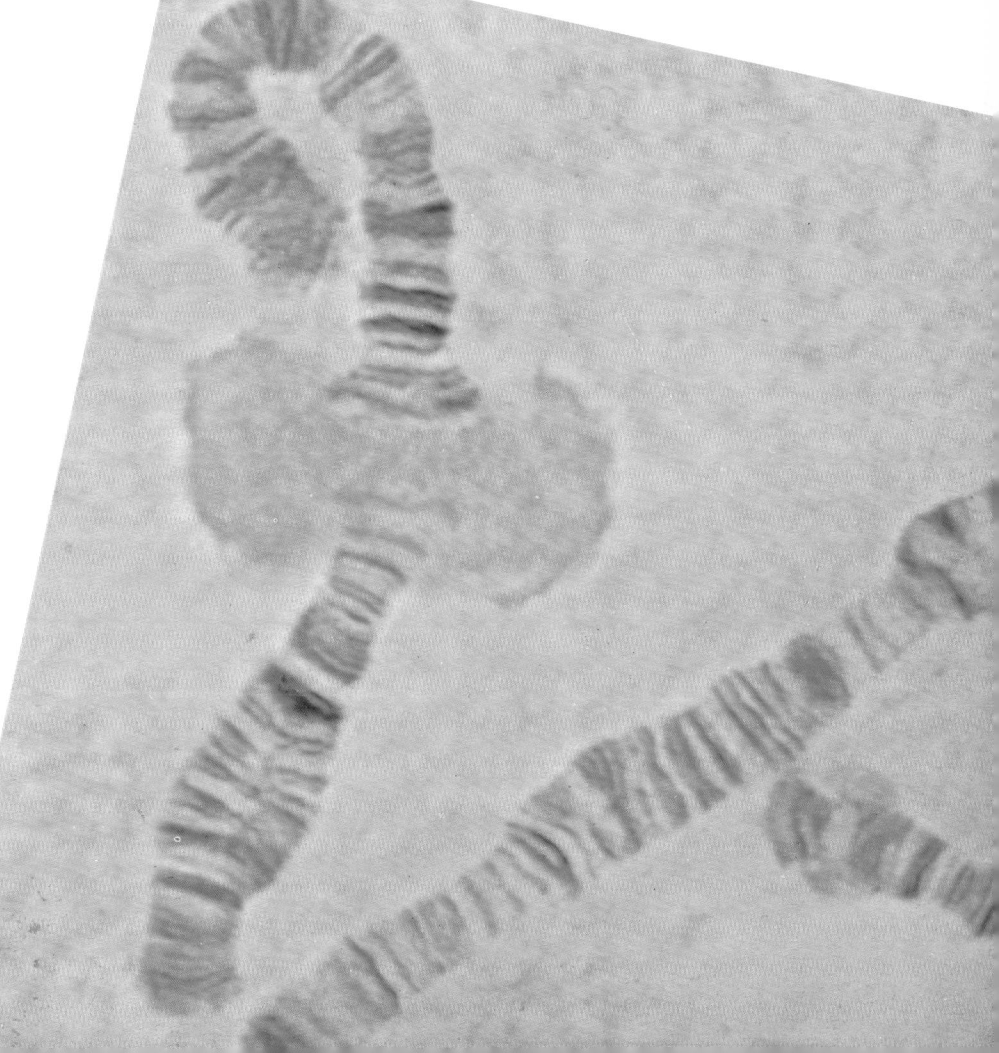

▼ These 'belts' are chromosomes from a midge's salivary glands, magnified 1,000 times. The dark bands are the genes. Genes occur in every living thing. They control its shape and structure.

CHROMATOGRAPHY

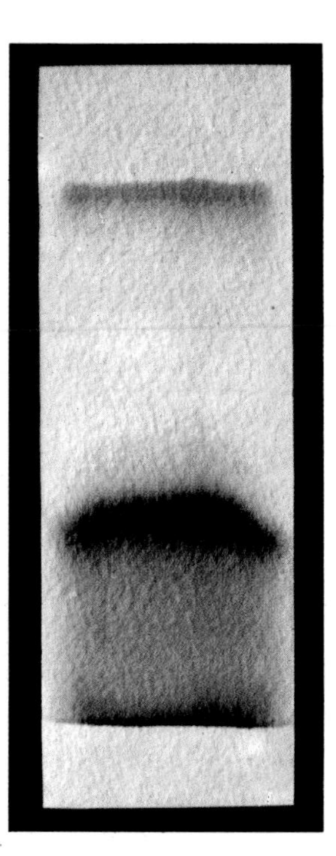

◀ Here a solvent substance has soaked up through paper, taking with it the mixture to be separated. Bands of colour show where separation occurred. This is the result of the type of experiment shown in the diagram **below**.

▶ Chromatography apparatus in a laboratory. The different colours in this column show different ingredients separating from a mixture.

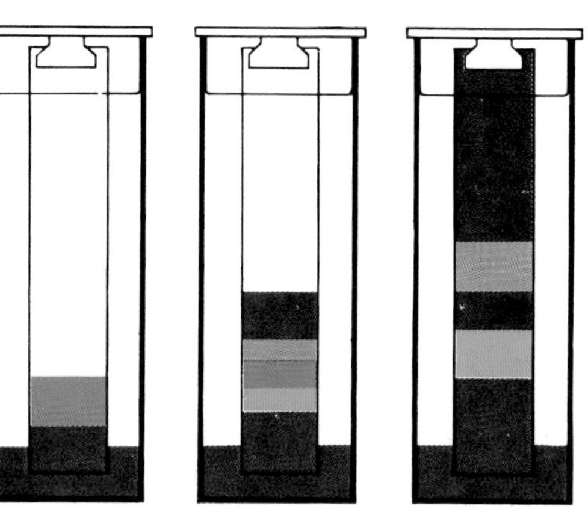

▶ This diagram shows how paper chromatography works. One end of a damp filter paper is dipped in a mixture (blue) and then hung in a jar containing solvent (grey). As the paper soaks up the solvent this takes with it particles from the mixture. One ingredient (turquoise) climbs more slowly than the other (mauve). In time both are separate.

Suppose you were a scientist wanting to separate the substances in plant sap, or to measure the dissolved gases in a sample of blood. At one time such tasks seemed quite impossible. Now, *chromatography* can help make them easy. Chromatography is a group of ways of separating the different chemicals in a mixture. The name chromatography means 'colour writing'.

How chromatography began

The first man to describe chromatography was the Russian botanist, Mikhail Tswett, in 1906. Tswett was trying to separate the pigments, or colouring matter, in green leaves. He dissolved the pigments in a solution. Then he poured it into a tube packed with powdered chalk. Tswett found that some pigments soaked into the chalk quickly. Others travelled farther down the tube before they stopped. So the different pigments produced bands of different colours. What Tswett had discovered was called adsorption chromatography. (Adsorption is what happens when one substance, such as chalk, attracts the molecules of another to its surface.)

Different kinds of chromatography

Tswett's experiment had separated dissolved solid substances. Other scientists developed his ideas and now other kinds of chromatography deal with other forms of matter. For instance, gas chromatography can separate a mixture made of different gases. In gas chromatography, a moving stream of gas carries a mixture of other gases up through a tube filled with a liquid or a solid substance. Different gases in the mixture travel through the tube at different rates. Those that travel fastest reach the top first. Those that are most slowed down by the liquid or the solid come out last. Each gas can be collected as it leaves the tube.

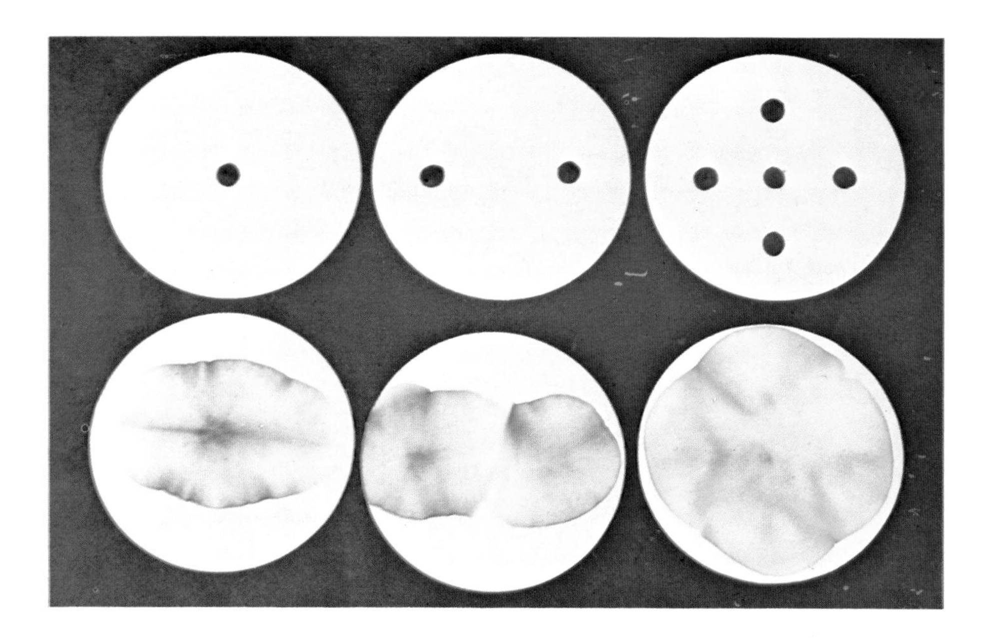

◀ Ink drops on damp filter paper (top row) act like this (bottom row) when you drip water on them. Some chemicals in ink spread faster than others. Different chemicals produce different colours.

SOAP

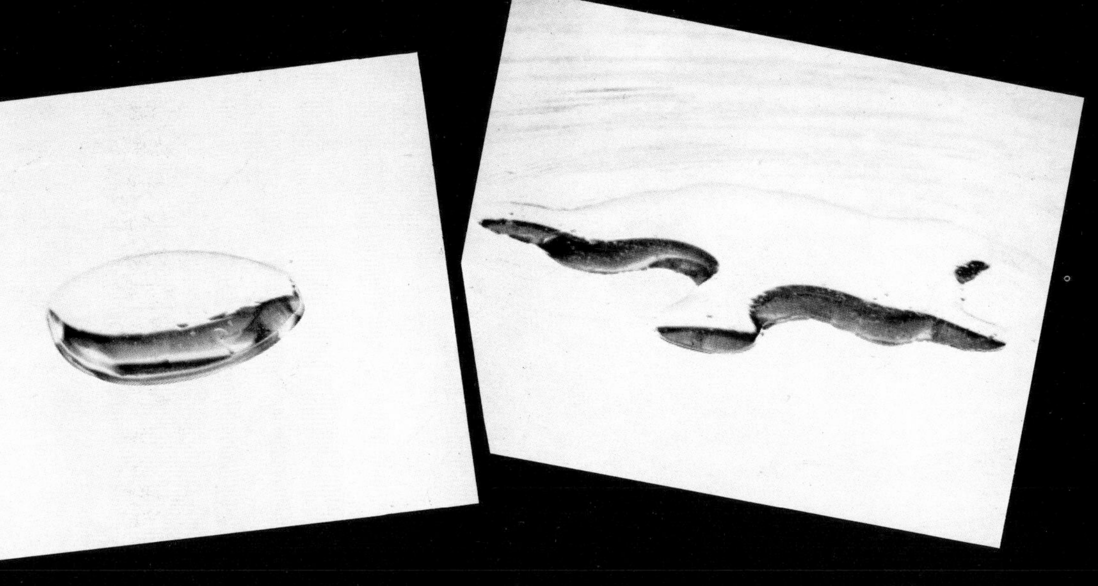

Far left: Pure water on a surface forms a droplet because a force called surface tension pulls the water molecules together. **Left:** Adding soap to the droplet reduces its surface tension, so the droplet collapses and the water spreads out.

Imagine using a metal instrument to scrap your skin clean after a bath. Greeks and Romans used to do this before everyone used soap instead. Try washing greasy plates in plain hot water. The grease sticks firmly to the plates. Add soap, and the grease lifts off easily. Without soap everyday life would be much dirtier and much more uncomfortable.

Legend has it that soap-making started on Sapo Hill near Rome some 1500 years ago. Peasants supposedly burnt animals as offerings to gods. The hot animal fat melted and soaked down through the ash from the fire into the clayey soil. People found that this soapy clay was good for washing clothes – or so the story goes.

People still make soap from animal fats, but vegetable oils are used as well. Oils are fats that stay liquid at room temperature. Fat contains fatty acids. To make soap, fat is boiled for hours with sodium hydroxide (caustic soda) or potassium hydroxide. Such chemicals are known as *alkalis*. Manufacturers add perfumes to give their soaps a pleasant smell. Many also add chemicals to kill harmful germs that can live on skin.

Why soap cleans

Soap cleans well because of the way its particles, or molecules, behave. One end of each soap molecule tends to stick to water. The other end 'hates' water but sticks to oil and grease. This has two effects. Soap molecules tend to pull apart the water molecules that form a kind of 'skin' at the water's surface. When its molecules are loosened in this way, water will wet plates and cups more thoroughly, so making them easier to clean. Soap also acts directly on grease and oily dirt. It breaks these into tiny droplets that you can simply rinse away.

Detergents

Soaps, and other substances that clean like soap, are called detergents. Special processes produce *synthetic* detergents. You find these in many washing powders and dish-washing liquids. Synthetic detergents can penetrate dirt more deeply than soap. Hard water contains chemicals that form a scum with soap and stop it cleaning properly. Synthetic detergents clean well in almost any kind of water.

▼ These diagrams show how soap and other detergents work. Molecules of soap have a water-loving 'head' and a water-hating 'tail'.
1 As soap dissolves, its 'tails' push water molecules apart. This helps soap to spread.
2 Tails stick to dirt particles on a fabric being washed. Shaking frees the dirt.
3 Soap particles hold dirt particles suspended in the water, and can be rinsed away.

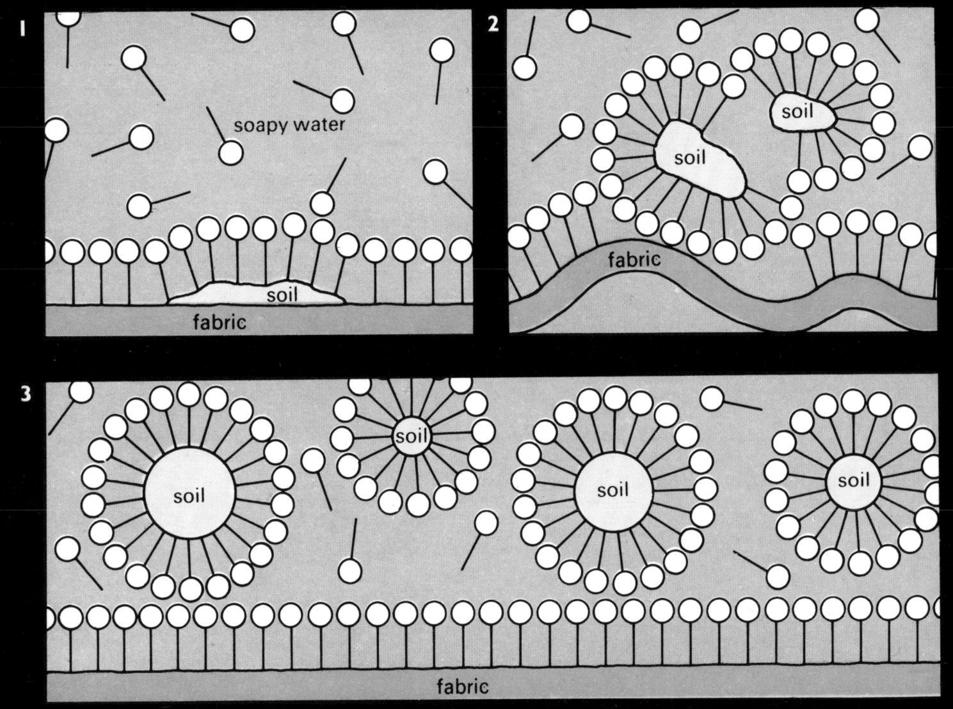

CEREALS

► Grains of barley have a different appearance from wheat grains. Many grow on slender spikes ending in long bristles. People feed barley to farm animals and use it for making beer.

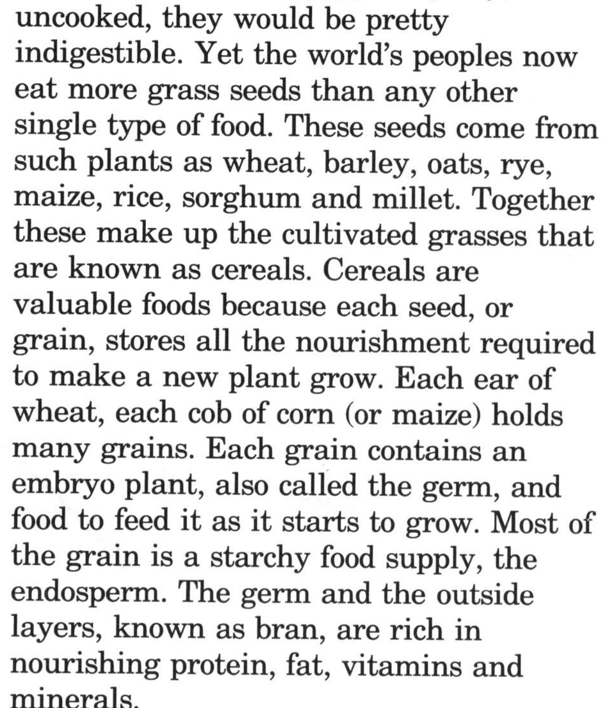

Take a handful of grass seeds. Look at them closely. These small objects scarcely seem a useful food supply. Anyway, uncooked, they would be pretty indigestible. Yet the world's peoples now eat more grass seeds than any other single type of food. These seeds come from such plants as wheat, barley, oats, rye, maize, rice, sorghum and millet. Together these make up the cultivated grasses that are known as cereals. Cereals are valuable foods because each seed, or grain, stores all the nourishment required to make a new plant grow. Each ear of wheat, each cob of corn (or maize) holds many grains. Each grain contains an embryo plant, also called the germ, and food to feed it as it starts to grow. Most of the grain is a starchy food supply, the endosperm. The germ and the outside layers, known as bran, are rich in nourishing protein, fat, vitamins and minerals.

The first grain growers

Our Stone Age ancestors knew none of this, yet by 10,00 years ago peoples in different parts of Asia were finding it worthwhile to harvest wild crops of wheat or rice – and even to plant them. No one knows just how this started. Perhaps a wandering family of hunters found a patch of land where grasses grew abundantly. They ate well. Before they

◄ Combine harvesters are called this because as they travel through a field of wheat they combine what used to be several separate time-consuming tasks. They cut the stalks of the crop and separate the grains from the unwanted husks.

◄ These ripe grains of wheat have been separated from the heads (or spikes or ears) where they grow on the wheat stalks. A mill will grind the grains into flour, for use in foods such as bread.

left they might have scattered seeds in thanks to the gods of growing things. The seeds sprouted thickly on that patch of land, so when the wanderers returned they found an even richer crop. This may be how people learnt to clear wild plants from plots of land and sow the soil with crops.

While men and women had had to hunt wild animals or gather wild plants to eat, finding food took almost all their time. Once people started cultivating cereals, one farmer's work produced enough to feed several people, who then had time for developing new skills. And so arts and crafts began. Indeed, growing cereals was the main discovery that made civilization possible.

Different ways of cultivation

Cereal growing spread around the world – wherever soils and climates proved suitable. Take wheat for instance. In the northern hemisphere, people have persuaded wheat to grow as far north as the Arctic Circle and as far south as the Equator. On dry lands they learnt to plant it every other year and leave the soil unplanted in the year between, to gather moisture. In wetter areas some people plant wheat every other year with a different crop in the year between. This crop rotation gives time for the soil to rebuild nutrients of the kinds that wheat has taken out. But farmers who feed the soil with fertilizer can grow wheat on the same fields year after year.

New machinery and know-how

In the world's richer countries machines do all the work of growing cereals and harvesting their grains. For instance, grain drills cut into soil and spread seeds evenly, then cover them with soil. This gives a thicker, more even crop than old methods of sowing seed by hand. Combine harvesters cut stalks, thresh grains from the ears (heads) of wheat and pour the grains into trucks. In the United States a farm worker can now cultivate more than 16 times as much land as his ancestor 100 years ago, before the development of modern farm machinery.

New knowledge is helping cereal production in other ways as well. Scientists are constantly developing new varieties of cereal. Some give higher yields than old-established strains, others can resist diseases or grow in harsh climates. For example, one short-stemmed strain of wheat carries a heavier ear of grain than older long-stemmed strains. It also withstands gales and rainstorms better.

The varieties of rice and other cereals have increased many countries' grain production enormously. Some nations that once had to buy grain from abroad now grow more than they need. But the world's population could increase faster than the grain crops that feed it, so scientists will have to keep on seeking ways to step up cereal production.

▲ Oats were once an important cereal crop in northern countries where the summer was too short for wheat to ripen. Now it is mainly used as animal feed.

▼ Rice grows on terraced hillsides here in the Philippines. Terraces make good use of steep slopes, and low mud walls trap monsoon rain. Rice needs a great deal of moisture while it is growing.

CERAMICS

'Ceramics' comes from a Greek word meaning potter's clay. Ceramics include many substances produced by being heated to a high temperature in a special oven called a kiln. But what happened before there were kilns? No one knows, but perhaps something like this happened. Long ago, some Stone Age peoples lined woven baskets with wet clay to make them waterproof. One day one of these baskets was accidentally dropped in the fire. The flames burnt the basketwork away, but baked the clay rock-hard. This could be the way in which people discovered how to turn soft wet clay into hard strong earthenware pots for use in storing food or water.

▼ This Greek potter is making earthenware pots on a low wheel. Potters in Mediterranean countries have been shaping urns like this for several thousand years.

Inventing better pots

In time people learnt to build up pots from 'worm'-like clay strips. By 5,000 years ago some Middle Eastern craftsmen were using their thumbs and fingers to shape pots quickly from clay lumps whirling around on a spinning potter's wheel. By baking, or firing, pots in a very hot kiln, potters produced harder pots than those which had been hardened in an open fire.

Water gradually soaks out through tiny pores in ordinary earthenware pots. To stop this potters learnt to paint earthenware with a special coat called a glaze. Inside the kilns the glaze formed a glassy, waterproof surface. Glazed pots were no longer porous, so liquids stored inside them could not leak out.

Porcelain

By 1,800 years ago the Chinese were using porcelain. This is a lovely, thin, hard, almost see-through kind of pottery. The Chinese made it from a special kind of clay fired at great heat. In time porcelain cups and bowls reached Europe. European potters trying to imitate porcelain made a new kind of pottery that they called 'china' after the porcelain

► A porcelain figure made by the great craftsman J Kändler who worked at the Meissen porcelain factory in the 1750s.

from China. But it was not until the eighteenth century that Europeans managed to make true porcelain. At Meissen, in what is now East Germany, craftsmen made lovely decorated dishes and small model human figures out of porcelain. Look out for examples of Meissen porcelain when you next visit a museum.

Ceramics have many uses in or near our homes. For instance, wash-basins are made of pottery. Their shiny glaze stops water leaking out. The bricks from which many homes are built are ceramics, too. So are the drainage pipes that carry waste water underground.

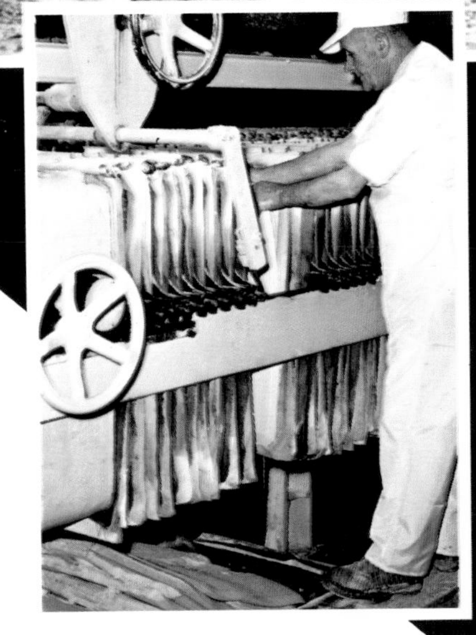

Four stages in making china.
Top A water jet loosens china clay from the walls of a quarry.
Left Presses squeeze water from the clay to make it usable.
Below A potter shapes a clay vase on a spinning wheel.
Bottom Infra-red heaters dry newly-glazed plates as they move along a production line.

Heat-proof ceramics

Some ceramics are made especially to withstand intense heat. For instance, you can safely roast food in oven-ware placed inside an oven hot enough to crack ordinary pottery. Fireclay bricks made from a special kind of clay are used to line the walls of kilns, where heat would make ordinary clay bricks burst. *Technologists* call such super heat-resisting ceramics 'refractories'. Jet engines and nuclear reactors contain refractory ceramics that will not melt or crack even at 5000° Centigrade – a temperature only a little cooler than the Sun's surface. But these refractories are not made of ordinary pottery clay. They are made from special substances such as alumina or silica. The kilns in which they are fired are heated by glowing 'arcs' of hot air produced by an electric current. (The temperature is so high that a metal heating element would melt.)

Suppose no one had invented paper. Instead of writing with ink on paper you might be using a sharp reed to make marks on soft clay tablets. That's how people wrote 5,500 years ago, soon after writing was invented. They baked the clay to harden it. Then they stored their baked clay 'books' in libraries.

Imagine how many tablets you might need to write down just one story. Think how awkward books like these would be to keep and move around. No wonder people gradually learnt to write on materials that were lighter and thinner than clay. These substances have included skins or parchment, bamboo, cloth, silk and tree bark. The ancient Egyptians cut reed into strips and pressed them together into sheets to write on.

How paper-making began

We get our word 'paper' from the papyrus reeds that the Egyptians used. But paper was invented later, and in China not in Egypt. Legend has it that the inventor was a Chinese government minister called Ts'ai Lun. In AD 105, the story goes, Ts'ai Lun found a way of treating tree bark to separate its fibres. Then he pounded or matted them into a sheet of paper. Later, the Chinese learnt to make paper by pounding down old fish nets, hemp, and even rags into thin sheets. Gradually, Chinese paper-making methods spread around the world.

Paper is still made from fibres. These are mostly cellulose (page 28) obtained from trees, grasses or other plants. Most paper comes from wood. Paper-makers prepare the fibres in a special form called pulp. Pulp is a soft mass of fibres mixed with water which is spread evenly onto a level surface such as a wire screen. Then the water drains away. This leaves a layer of fibres on the surface. The fibres stick together to produce a thin sheet. This sheet is paper.

For centuries all paper was made by hand – a slow process. But in 1750, a new Dutch machine speeded up the task of breaking rags into fibres. Then, in 1798, a French inventor called Nicholas Robert produced a machine that made paper in long rolls.

Paper-making today

Today paper is still made in rolls, but in huge paper mills capable of producing paper at 800m ($\frac{1}{2}$ mile) a minute, in sheets up to 10m (30ft) wide. The paper from such factories goes into books, newspapers, toilet rolls and many other objects made of paper. Only mass-production methods can produce enough of it. Every year each American alone, on average, uses more than 200kg (450lb) of paper articles. The world's demand for paper is immense.

◄ Three stages in the production of paper. Lumberjacks fell the trees with chain-saws. The tree trunks are dragged to the nearest river where they are floated downstream to a paper mill. At the mill they are taken from the water and the bark stripped off before the pulping process begins.

▼ The interior of a paper mill, showing the huge rolls of paper that will be used to make all the different paper products that we use every day.

PRINTING

In many countries almost everyone can learn to read and write. This is largely because books are plentiful and cheap. In the Middle Ages few people could read or write. The main reason was that books were scarce and costly. In fact few people could afford to buy one. There were two reasons for this. First, books were made from expensive sheets of parchment. Second, each book had to be copied out by hand. This was a slow process, as copying one volume could take months; 45 clerks spent almost 2 years producing 200 volumes for an Italian prince.

By the 1400s two inventions had begun to change all this. The two were paper (page 22) and printing. Printing probably began in China. First, the Chinese learnt to stamp goods with seals that bore their owners' marks. Later, Chinese people stamped colourful designs on playing cards and pictures on wooden blocks. They could print a page of text by simply inking a carved block and pressing it upon a sheet of paper.

Chinese discoveries like these spread west to Europe. By the early 1400s Europeans were making whole books by wood-block printing. But this meant separately carving every letter of each word. So making books was still a slow and costly process. Then, about 1440, a craftsman made a startling invention. He mass-produced letter shapes that could be moved around. A printer could use these shapes to build words for one book, then separate the letters and re-use them for another book. Such letter shapes are known as movable type.

A goldsmith, Johann Gutenberg of Germany, ran the first big printing firm to work in this way. Gutenberg used a goldsmith's tools to punch letter shapes in soft metal. With his fingers he would pick up the letters one by one, arranging them in rows to make a page of type held together by a frame. Gutenberg then marked the type surface with a special sticky ink applied by a leather ink ball. Lastly, he pressed the type onto a sheet of paper. For this he used a wine press of the kind then used for crushing grapes. When Gutenberg removed the paper sheet it was a printed page.

All these advances speeded up the printing process, although it was very slow by modern printing standards.

► This 16th-century picture shows a printer at work using his hand-operated printing press. The three smartly dressed men on the left are looking at some of the books he has already printed.

Speeding up the presses

Many further inventions have helped speed up the rate of the printing process. First, the wooden presses were replaced with stronger, more powerful presses of cast iron. Then came the idea of rolling a heavy metal cylinder over the paper instead of pressing a block onto it. In London, in 1814, came another improvement. 'The Times' newspaper was printed with a cylinder press in which both cylinder and type 'bed' moved, but in opposite directions.

In 1835 came the first rotary press, where type locked onto one cylinder was rolled against another. Paper fed between both rollers came out printed. Meanwhile steam power speeded up the process even more. A steam engine could drive a printing press much faster than one worked by hand. Steam power helped to make it possible to mass-produce a newspaper each night. For instance, take composing – setting up the lines of type. Until the 1880s this task was very laborious. The compositor had to pick up each individual letter and place it in position – just as Gutenberg had done 400 years earlier. But with the invention of the linotype (line-of-type) machine in the 1890s composing could be done mechanically – so making it much faster.

Four printing processes

Centuries of invention have produced four basic processes for printing ink on paper. The four are letterpress, gravure, lithography and screen printing. In letterpress, ink coats the raised surface of the type. In gravure, ink coats the surface of a metal plate. A blade scrapes off all ink except that filling shallow hollows in the plate. That ink is then transferred to paper. In lithography ink sticks to greasy areas on a printing plate, but not to areas made wet with water. In screen printing, the printer makes a wax or plastic stencil on top of a screen of metal gauze or silk. Then he inks the screen. Where there is no wax or plastic, the ink spreads through to paper below. The printer can use different inks with different stencils to produce one multi-coloured print. Screen printing is a simple and popular method of printing posters.

▶ The full-colour picture of a butterfly was made by printing four different inks from four printing plates over one another. The plates were made by photographing the original picture through filters that picked out in turn its yellow, magenta (a red) and cyan (a blue). It was also photographed in black and white. In printing, all colours can be made from yellow, magenta and cyan. Black gives extra clarity.

◀ And this is what a printing works looks like today! Machines do everything except make the occasional quality check. In the background on the left you can see a printing press that can print many pages at once. The magazine is folded in the machine on the right, the cover is then stapled or stitched on and finally the magazine is carried by the conveyor belt to the despatch department where it will be sent off to customers.

TEXTILES

▼ A knitting machine makes one leg of a pair of tights. Knitting machines like this use rows of needles that move up and down on a rounded frame.

Imagine a world where people wore nothing but leaves or the skins of animals, and homes lacked carpets, cushions, curtains, sheets or blankets. That's what life was like before textiles were invented.

What are textiles?
Textiles are woven materials – that is they are made by interlacing threads of fibrous substances. Natural fibres used for making textiles include cotton, linen, silk and wool. Man-made fibres include rayon,

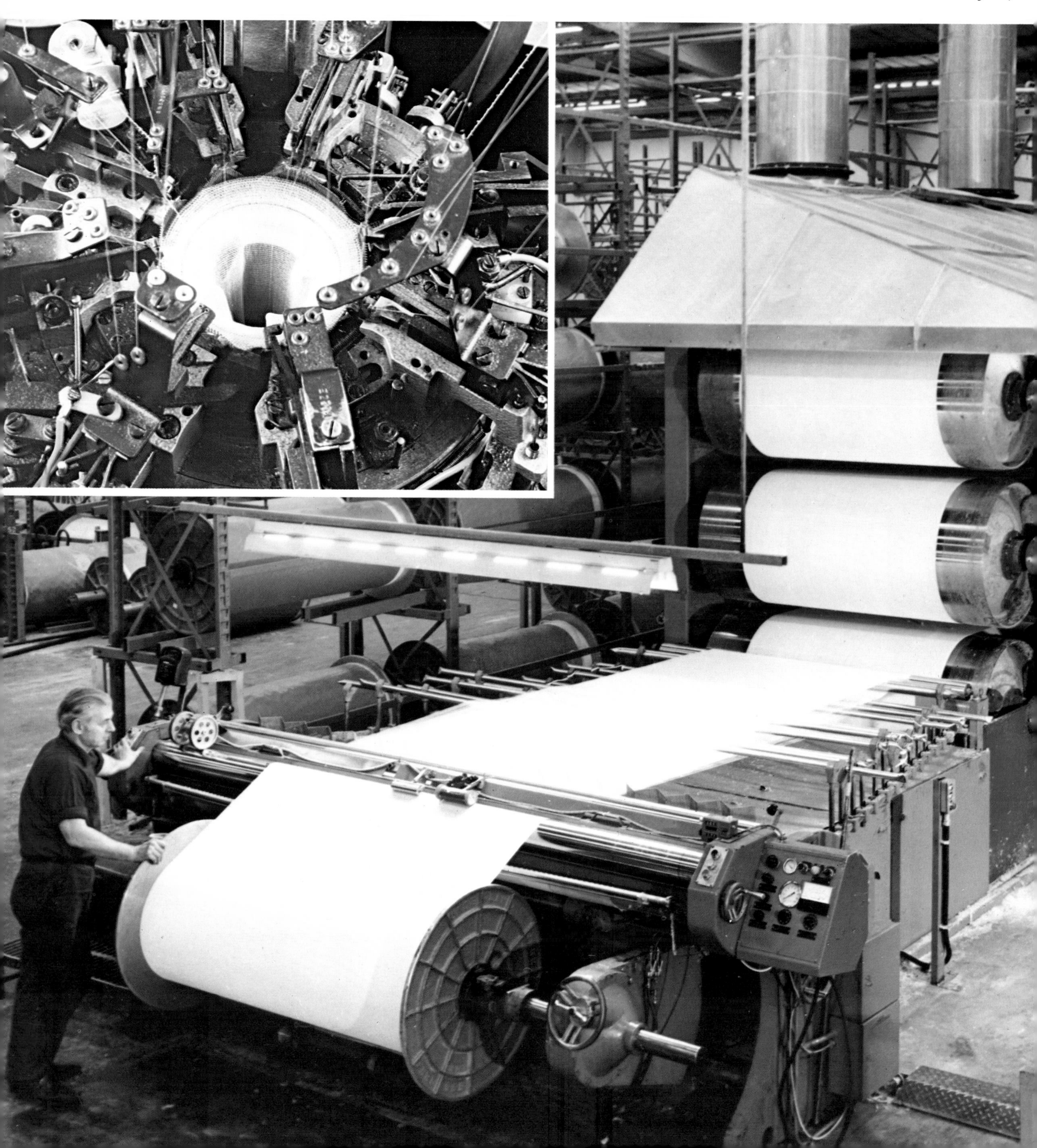

▼ The sizing department of a textile mill coats rolls of yarn with a paste called size. This holds the fibres together and strengthens the yarn for weaving. Size is what makes a new tea towel feel stiff.

nylon, acrylic and polyester. Besides clothes and soft furnishings, textiles provide us with bandages, flags, parachutes, sails, typewriter ribbons, and many, many other useful articles.

Early textile-making

No one knows just when or where someone first discovered how to make textiles. Perhaps in the Stone Age people learnt to weave long grass stems into mats and baskets. Among the first known textiles are linen cloths woven by ancient Egyptian craftsmen, perhaps 6,000 years ago, to wrap around the bodies of the dead.

Most natural fibres are short strands that must be twisted together, or spun, to make long threads, called yarn. People used to spin yarn by pulling strands from a ball of fibres, twisting them between their fingers as they did so. The earliest weaving was done on a simple hand loom. The weaver stretched strands of spun yarn tightly between two pieces of wood that formed the frame; then threaded other strands over and under the first strands. (Yarn forming the length of a fabric is called the warp. Yarn threaded across the warp is called the weft, or filling.)

Textile making was a slow task while people operated all machinery by hand. But in the eighteenth century British inventors found ways of producing large quantities of cotton very quickly. First, in 1733, John Kay invented a so-called flying shuttle to speed the weft thread's journeys back and forth. Later, Richard Arkwright made a mechanical spinning frame that spun vast amounts of yarn. Soon, steam-powered machines were weaving textiles far faster than was possible by hand. Now, textiles can be mass-produced so cheaply that almost everyone can afford to buy them.

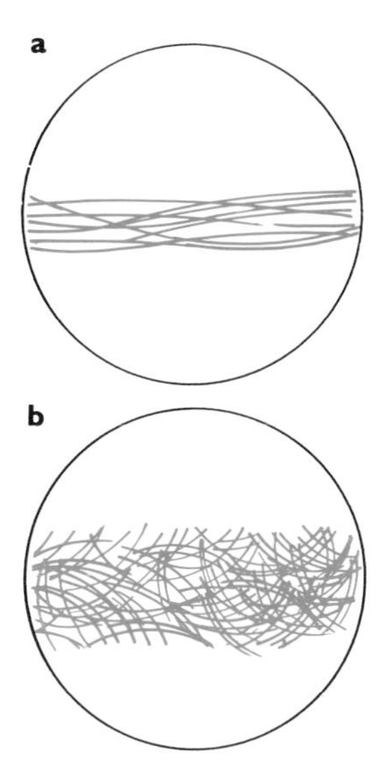

▲ Two kinds of thread are shown here magnified.
a Thread made from long filaments of silk.
b Spun yarn – short strands of wool fibre twisted together to make one long strand.

▼ These are the main parts of a simple loom for weaving cloth by hand. Heddle rods lift alternate warp strands (shown as red and blue). The weft strand is wound onto the shuttle which takes the weft between the parted strands. Then these close, to hold the weft between them. Next, warp strands part again, in the opposite direction, and the shuttle travels back between them.

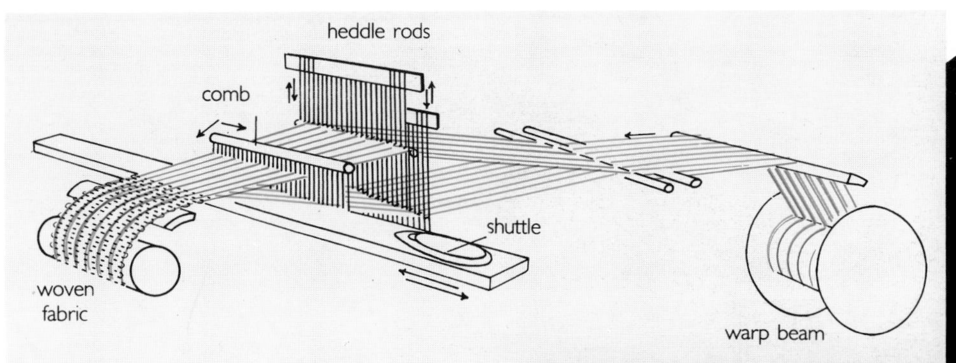

CELLULOSE

Walk through a wood or meadow and you are surrounded by the substance known as *cellulose*. Trees, grass and other plants are largely made of cellulose. For cellulose is the main ingredient in the cell walls that form plants' building blocks. Indeed cellulose makes up one-third of the weight of all the world's vegetable matter.

People began making use of cellulose long before they knew that such a thing existed. Stone Age men were using cellulose when they made wooden spears and hunting bows. Thousands of years ago people in hot countries learnt to weave cool cotton clothes from cotton fibres, which are mostly cellulose. Now cellulose has many other uses, for example in newsprint, certain plastics and explosives.

What is cellulose?

Fresh inventions became possible in the nineteenth century as chemists worked out what cellulose is made of. We now know that cellulose is a *carbohydrate* – a chemical compound containing atoms of carbon, hydrogen and oxygen. Each molecule of cellulose is very large, and built up of smaller molecules of a sugar known as glucose. These smaller molecules link up in a long chain to form each molecule of cellulose. These long-chain molecules help to make a plant strong and yet elastic, so that it bends but does not snap.

In the nineteenth century, chemists

▼ A worker checking a machine that packs cellulose fibre into bales for making rayon. The fibre comes in different thicknesses for making textiles of different weights and strengths.

▲ This syrupy stuff is cellulose used for making the artificial fibre rayon. The cellulose came from plant material treated with special chemicals.

were learning how to separate cellulose from other substances in plants. By the 1870s inventors were finding ways of boiling wood chips with special chemicals to remove unwanted substances and leave the cellulose. Nowadays, wood pulp is mostly used for making paper. Large quantities of cellulose provide us with our daily newspapers.

Nitrocellulose and celluloid

Once it was possible to collect pure cellulose from plants inventors found several ways of using it. Most methods involve breaking down the cellulose molecules and replacing parts of them with other groups of chemicals. In this way inventors obtained entirely new materials. For instance, in 1846 the German chemist Christian Schönbein treated cellulose with nitric *acid* and produced nitrocellulose – a new and highly dangerous explosive. He and other chemists found that slightly different ingredients produced other, safer, useful kinds of nitrocellulose. Today, nitrocellulose lacquers are sprayed on cars, planes and furniture to form a hard, glossy surface.

In 1872 the American scientist Isaiah Hyatt gave the name celluloid to a substance made by heating cellulose and camphor under *pressure*. Celluloid was the first plastic used for making photographic film.

Rayon and cellophane

In 1884 the French inventor Hilaire Chardonnet claimed he could produce an artificial silk from cellulose. People later called this substance rayon. Chemists make rayon by treating wood or cotton with special chemicals to produce a liquid that is poured through tiny holes. It comes out as cellulose or cellulose acetate thread that can be woven and used for making textiles.

Yet another useful product made from cellulose is cellophane. This comes from cellulose fibres softened in a solution that is then passed through rollers to produce a thin, light, flexible see-through sheet. In 1908 the Swiss chemist Jacques Brandenberger developed a machine for making sheets of cellophane. Cellophane became an important airtight, waterproof packaging material for certain foods – the forerunner of today's plastic wrappings.

▲ Workers feed logs into machines that turn the logs into pulp. Cellulose obtained from pulp goes to make certain types of clothes and wrappings.

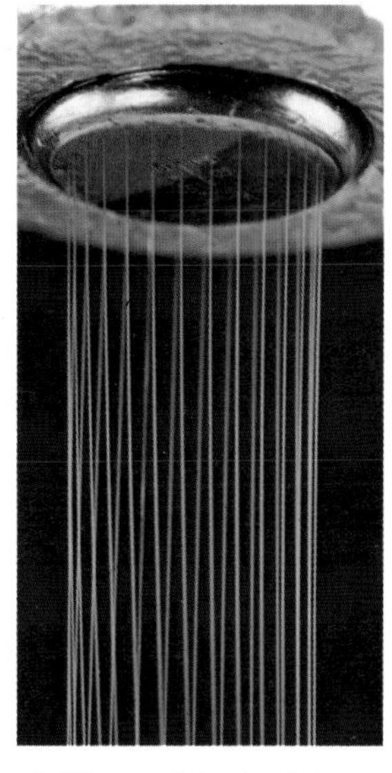

▲ These thin 'rods' are strands of cellulose acetate, being spun like natural yarn.

PLASTICS

► A radio made in the 1930s with a Bakelite case. Although it could be rather brittle, Bakelite was the first commercially successful synthetic plastic.

Many objects in and near your home are made of plastics. Dolls, mixing bowls, trousers, skirts, car tyres, buildings and aircraft all contain these hugely useful products. Many plastics look like glass, metal, wood or other natural substances. But plastics are all made by man. They come from simple substances like oil, air, methane gas and water.

Factories can produce plastics in almost any shape and shade. Some kinds are as hard as steel. Others are as soft as wool. Some melt in hot water. Others can resist a blow-torch flame.

All belong to one of two main groups – thermoplastics and thermosetting plastics. Thermoplastics can be melted and remoulded any number of times. Thermosetting plastics can be melted and moulded only once.

The first plastics

Inventors first produced plastics as cheap substitutes for natural materials. By the 1860s a British chemist, John Parkes, and an American scientist, John Wesley Hyatt (Isiah Hyatt's brother), had begun to manufacture 'natural' plastics from cellulose (page 28). In 1869, Hyatt invented celluloid ivory, for making billiard balls, in place of ivory. In 1884 the French chemist Hilaire Chardonnet invented the first man-made fibre, rayon. And the Swiss chemist Jacques Brandenberger developed cellophane. But all these plastics came largely from ready-made cellulose plant fibres. So, in a way, these plastics were only partly synthetic.

Synthetic plastics

Truly synthetic plastics are those that chemists can produce entirely from chemicals in a laboratory. They are now far more important than any other kind of plastic.

The first useful synthetic plastic was patented in 1909. Its name, Bakelite, comes from that of its developer, the Belgian-born American chemist Leo Baekeland. Baekeland mixed carbolic acid with formaldehyde, adding small amounts of other chemicals and heating them together under pressure. The result was a clear, hard substance that could be moulded into almost any shape, and was not damaged by chemicals or weather. Bakelite proved useful in making combs,

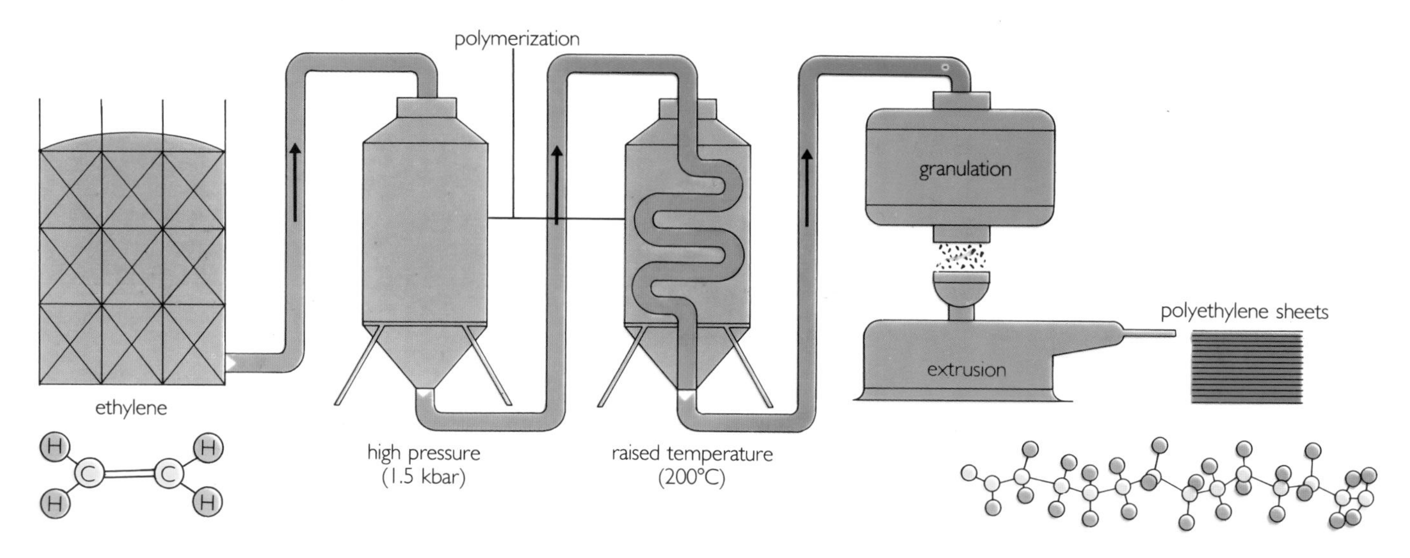

▼ Diagram to show how polyethylene is manufactured. High pressure and high temperatures cause ethylene molecules to form long chains called polymers. This process produces granules that can be extruded (squeezed) to form sheets of polyethylene.

electric insulators, light switches, radios and even engine parts. Bakelite was so successful that chemists quickly started trying to develop even better plastics. Among the best-known scientists was the American chemist Wallace Carothers. He took chemicals produced from coal, air and water. Then he rearranged the chemicals' molecules into long chains or solid networks as building blocks for making brand-new substances. (Such substances are known as *polymers* from Greek words meaning 'many parts'.) Between 1928 and 1934 Carothers developed nylon – one of the strongest, toughest, most elastic substances of all.

Modern plastics

Nylon is still among our most useful synthetic plastics, although many more have been invented. Thus acrylonitrile provides the soft, tough, springy, wool-like fibres of the fabric Acrilan. Butadiene gas is used to make synthetic rubber able to absorb shocks without cracking. Polystyrene is a hard, but brittle plastic used for radio and television casings. Chemists put all three together and made ABS, short for acrylonitrile-butadiene-styrene. This light, shatterproof substitute for metal is one of the toughest of all plastics. It serves for making almost anything from water pipes to boats and lorry bodies.

Early plastics were substitutes for natural products that were scarce or expensive. But some modern plastics meet needs no natural product ever satisfied. Among these new synthetics are the so-called fluorocarbon polymers, like Teflon, the non-stick substance used on saucepans and frying pans.

▲ Plastics are now highly sophisticated and can be adapted to many different uses. This Fiero from the Pontiac range of cars has a body of two different types of plastic, guaranteed to eliminate problems of rust.

▼ Telephone wires are now insulated with a protective coat of a plastic known as polyvinyl chloride – PVC for short.

► Part of a modern plastics factory. Here heavy-duty ridged PVC tubing is being made by a completely automatic process.

GLASS

Glass is hard, strong and waterproof and you can see through it. This makes it one of our most useful products. Glass windows let in light and help to keep in heat, but shut out chilly winds. We drink from glass tumblers. We store food in glass jars. Eyeglasses, or spectacles, help people with poor eyesight to see. Glass lenses magnify far-off stars and tiny living things that would be otherwise invisible. We depend on glass in many, many ways. Surprisingly, perhaps, the ingredients for glass are cheap and plentiful. Glass is mainly made from sand, soda and lime.

Early glassmaking

Nature has been making glass for many million years. Sometimes lightning hits sand and fuses (melts) it to form glass tubes. Volcanic eruptions may fuse rock and sands into obsidian, a glassy kind of stone. Stone Age hunters used obsidian for making knives and arrowheads long before people learnt to make glass for themselves. This happened several thousand years ago, probably by chance. According to one story the discoverers were merchants camping on a sandy shore in Syria. They propped their cooking pots over the camp fire on lumps of carbonate of soda, from their cargo. (Carbonate of soda is an alkali.) Next morning they found that the heat and alkali had melted some sand, producing lumps of glass. The tale is just a legend, but something like it could have happened. People first deliberately produced glass to put a shiny coat on beads. In Egypt people were glazing soapstone beads 6,000 years ago. By 4,500 years ago craftsmen were making small glass objects. A thousand years later came containers made of glass.

People made the first glass vessels by dipping a clay mould into molten glass

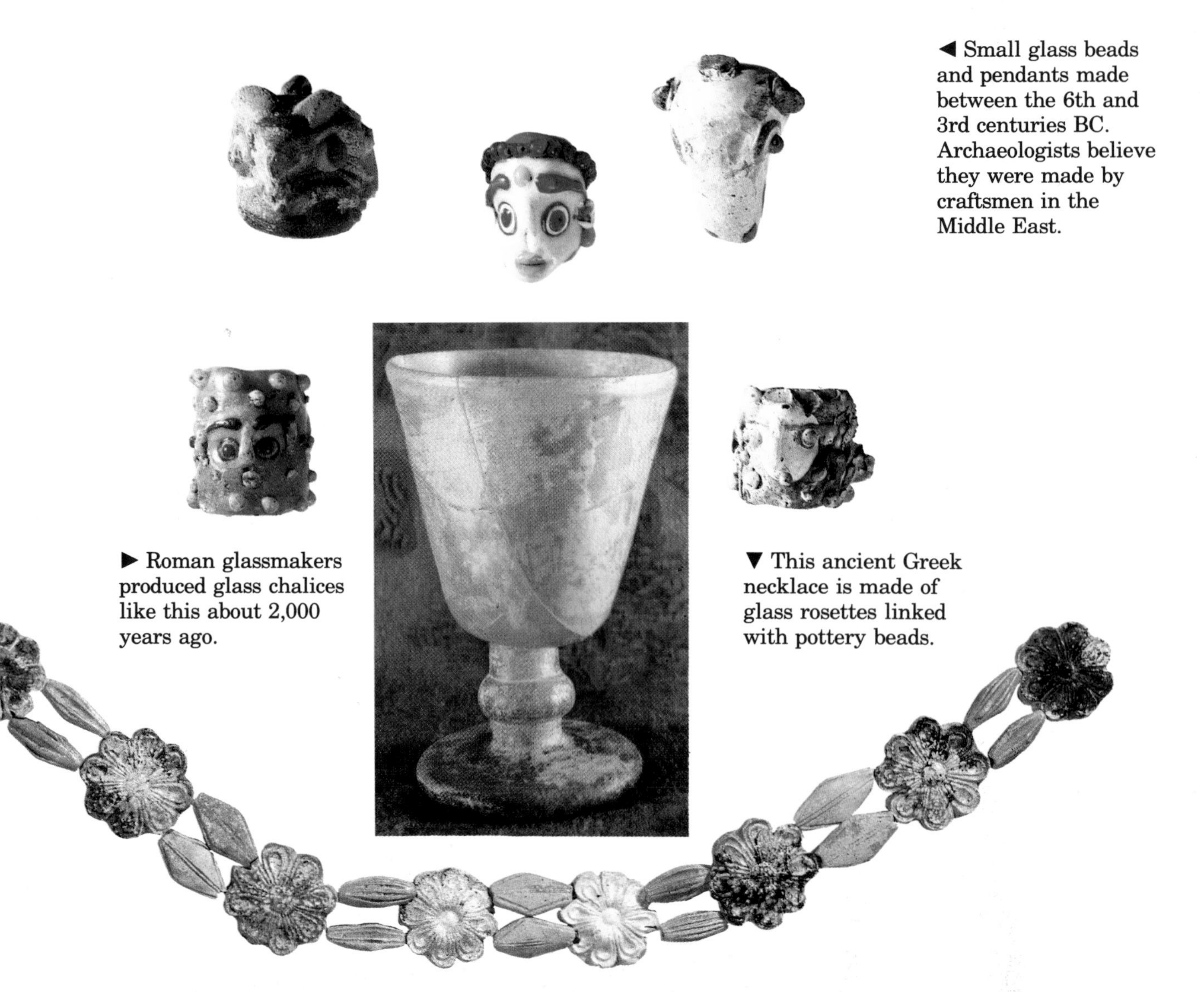

◀ Small glass beads and pendants made between the 6th and 3rd centuries BC. Archaeologists believe they were made by craftsmen in the Middle East.

► Roman glassmakers produced glass chalices like this about 2,000 years ago.

▼ This ancient Greek necklace is made of glass rosettes linked with pottery beads.

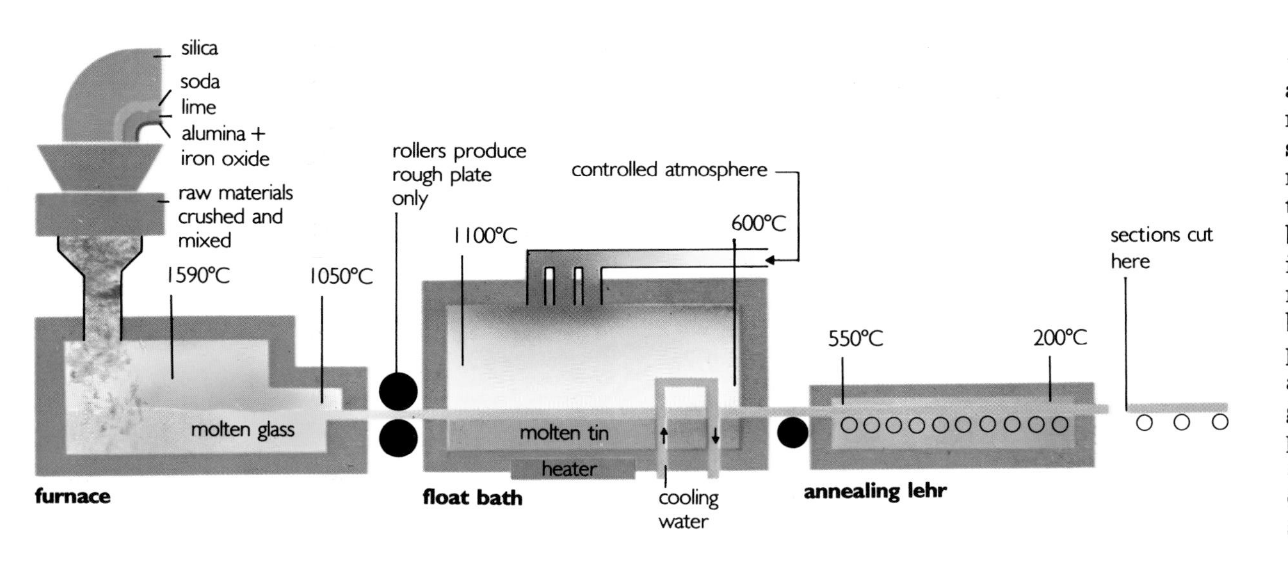

◀ The float process is an automatic way of making smooth glass sheets. From a furnace, red-hot glass is rolled to the right thickness between rollers. Then it floats on a bath of molten tin. This makes both surfaces flat and parallel. In the annealing lehr, the glass cools slowly to prevent cracking. Then automatic cutters made of diamonds cut it into sheets.

and letting it cool. About the first century BC some craftsmen learnt a quicker method. They collected a lump of molten glass as soft as toffee on one end of a long tube. Then they blew hard through the other end of the tube. This formed a bubble in the blob of molten glass. By twisting the tube so the blob of glass did not sag and then dipping the glass into water to cool it, the craftsman produced a glass container.

Modern glassmaking

Inventors have developed many ways of making glass. Most modern glass is mass-produced in factories. For instance, the raw materials for making glass jars are fed into a huge furnace. Molten glass flows out in a steady stream into moulds, where presses automatically force the glass into each cavity. Then the shaped glass is gradually cooled as it moves along a conveyor belt. Slow cooling (or *annealing*) prevents the jars from cracking.

Factories can add special ingredients to produce different types of glass suitable for different purposes. Lead oxide helps to put the sparkle in a wine glass. Boric oxide added in the making of some kitchen bowls prevents them cracking if they are cooled or heated quickly. Cobalt oxide colours glass deep blue. Craftsmen use such coloured glass to make the lovely stained-glass windows that you find in many churches.

▲ Burners keep a large newly made glass vessel hot and soft enough for final shaping by machines. Machines do almost all the work in many modern factories producing glass.

▼ Glassblowers blow air through blowpipes into blobs of molten glass that they have lifted from a furnace.

RUBBER

► Young rubber trees growing in a nursery. They will be carefully looked after until they are large enough to plant out in the main rubber plantations to replace old trees.

Stretch an elastic band and watch it spring back when you release one end. Notice how the soles and heels of sports shoes absorb shock when you walk. These and many other objects that you know are made of rubber. Tennis balls, pencil erasers, car shock absorbers and car tyres are just a few of more than 40,000 different rubber objects made in factories today.

Rubber serves many purposes because it is the most useful springy substance known. It is also airtight, tough, long-lasting, shock-absorbent and waterproof. No other known substance shares all these qualities.

Rubber comes in two forms: natural and man-made. American Indians used natural rubber many centuries before scientists invented synthetic rubber.

Discovering rubber

According to one story Christopher Columbus was the first European to see American Indians using rubber. This was in 1493, on his second voyage to America. On the island of Haiti (now Hispaniola), Columbus noticed some boys playing with a ball behaving like no ball that he had ever seen. When they threw it on the ground the ball bounced high in the air. When they squeezed it out of shape it sprang back into shape as soon as they let go.

Columbus found out how the ball was made. The local people cut holes in the bark of certain trees. A white milky liquid oozed out, then dried fast, becoming a dark, hard spongy solid.

Three centuries later, the English scientist Joseph Priestley discovered that this substance rubbed out pencil marks. So he called it 'rubber' – the name it bears today.

Natural rubber

At first, people saw natural rubber as little more than an amazing toy. This was because it suffered one major disadvantage. Cold weather made rubber products break easily, and great heat turned them sticky. In 1839 the American inventor Charles Goodyear made a chance discovery that changed all that. Goodyear accidentally spilled a sulphur–rubber mixture on a hot stove, and found that rubber treated in this way stayed firm and tough whatever the temperature. People called Goodyear's heat treatment vulcanization after Vulcan, the Romans' god of fire. Nowadays most natural rubber products are made from vulcanized rubber.

Natural rubber comes mainly from a tropical tree belonging to the castor-bean family. (The rubber plants you see in many houses are no relation.) Rubber trees grow wild in the Amazon forest region of Brazil. Brazil's wild rubber trees once provided almost all the world's rubber. But the trees grew far apart, which made collecting rubber slow and costly. Then, in the 1870s, British scientists shipped seedling Brazilian rubber trees to Ceylon and Malaya. People began to grow them in plantations there. Now most natural rubber comes from rubber trees grown outside Brazil.

Man-made rubber

In World War 1 the Allies prevented Germany obtaining rubber. The Germans badly needed rubber for the tyres of their army vehicles. So German chemists tried producing rubber artificially from chemicals. They knew that each rubber molecule is built of a long chain of smaller molecules of a substance called isoprene. They also knew that isoprene occurs not just in rubber but in natural

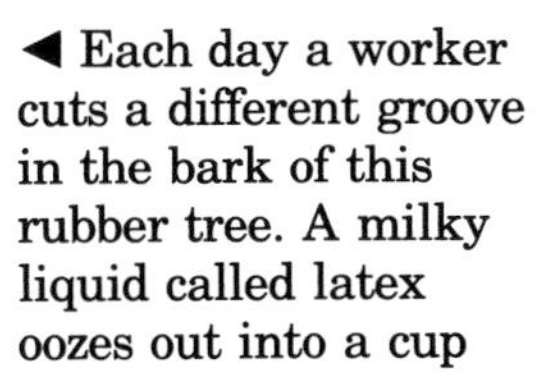

◀ Each day a worker cuts a different groove in the bark of this rubber tree. A milky liquid called latex oozes out into a cup (**below**). When he has tapped all down one side of the tree, the rubber tapper can take latex from the other.

gas, petroleum and turpentine. From such substances the chemists collected molecules of isoprene and tried linking them to make man-made rubber. At first they failed. But by World War 2 Germany and the United States were both producing large amounts of synthetic rubber. However, the first really good synthetic substitute for rubber first appeared in 1953, well after World War 2 ended. Now, most of the world's rubber is synthetic.

▼ Machines in this factory are making car and lorry tyres. Tyres made from a mixture of natural and synthetic rubbers are strong and wear well. But aircraft tyres are made from natural rubber, which gives a softer landing than synthetic rubber.

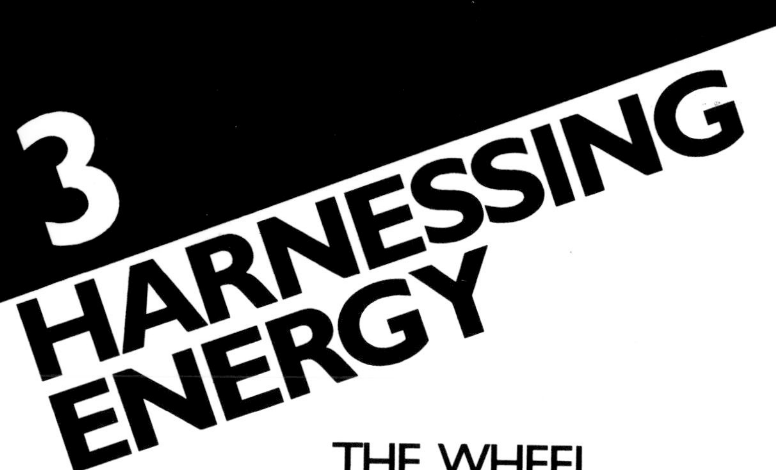

3 HARNESSING ENERGY

THE WHEEL

Some people think the wheel is mankind's greatest-ever invention. Without wheels we would still depend on legs to carry us around, and we would still be dragging loads on sleds.

Wheeled vehicles move over land more easily than sleds. Tiny roughnesses in the ground rub against the sliding runners of a sled. This friction slows down the sled. Wheels do not slide, they roll. So there is little friction where the wheel's rim meets the ground.

How wheels began

Someone invented the wheel at least 5,500 years ago, but we do not know where or when. Perhaps the idea grew after people started moving huge stones by resting them on logs, then by rolling the logs along. The ancient Egyptians and ancient Britons used log rollers in this way. But they found that their loads kept sliding forward, off the logs.

Then an ingenious person solved the problem be pegging together three flat

▼ Mexican women use this wheel to spin yarn for weaving cloth. One woman turns the wheel by hand. A belt fixed to the wheel turns a spindle that winds wool or cotton fibres into yarn.

► French wheelwrights add an iron tyre to a cart wheel's wooden rim to protect it from wear. They fit the tyre while it is hot, then add cold water to cool and shrink the iron. This makes it grip the wheel more tightly.

◀ This four-wheeled 'Moon buggy' helped astronauts explore the Moon. Only a little air was needed to blow up its tyres, for the Moon has no atmosphere to push them inward.

▼ Wheels can go over all kinds of surface on land or on the Moon. This 'beach buggy' has specially wide tyres to help it travel on deep sand.

pieces of wood to form a solid disc. This wheel turned on a long rounded pole called an axle. One end of the axle went through a hole in the middle of the wheel. There were two wheels to each axle and two axles were fixed crosswise, perhaps to the underneath of a sled. When this sled with wheels was pulled, the wheels turned but the fixed axles did not. So a load did not fall off as it would have fallen off log rollers.

Improving the wheel

Solid wheels were strong but heavy, and wagons with these wheels were slow. But by 2,000 BC people were replacing solid wheels with spoked wheels, which were much lighter. Spokes are thin rods or sticks. They join the wheel's outside edge, the rim, to its strong centre, or hub. Spoked wheels were first used for speedy, two-wheeled war chariots.

By the 1830s engineers were designing wheels big enough and strong enough to carry steam-powered railway locomotives. These wheels were made of iron instead of wood. The metal wheels of trains gave a smooth ride, for they rolled along level metal rails. But most roads were bumpier than railway tracks. All-metal wheels proved too hard to 'cushion' road passengers from bumps. This problem was solved when rubber tyres for cars were developed in the 1880s. Rubber is strong and tough but softer and springier than wood or metal. So rubber cushions bumps well. Nowadays, car tyres have only an outer covering of rubber. Inside they are entirely filled with air. Pneumatic tyres like these give an even softer ride than solid rubber tyres.

Other kinds of wheel

Wheels have many uses besides those described above. For instance, a wheel and axle can be used for lifting heavy weights. Gear wheels inside a car help the driver transfer movement from the engine to the main wheels. *Gears* are wheels that turn metal axles. Each gear wheel has teeth around the rim. One gear wheel's teeth fit into another's, so one gear wheel turns another and its axle.

GRAVITATION

If you hold a heavy stone in your hand, you feel a force that tries to pull it down toward the ground. If you release the stone, it falls. That's obvious, it always happens. But why? For thousands of years no one could provide an answer. Nor could anyone explain why air and water cling to the surface of our spinning Earth instead of flying off.

Newton's theory
In 1687, the English scientist Sir Isaac Newton came up with an answer to these and other questions. According to an old story, Newton had been drinking tea in his garden when he saw an apple drop from a tree. At once he saw there was just one reason why objects fall to Earth, why the Moon stays orbiting the Earth, and why the Earth stays orbiting the Sun. Newton worked out that all matter, from an atom to a star, exerts a pulling force on all other matter in the universe. This pull is *gravitation*. Newton found that the strength of gravitation depends on two things: *mass* and distance. Mass is the amount of matter in an object. The greater an object's mass, the greater its pulling power on other objects.

▼ Gravity pulls this parachutist down to Earth. Only the way his parachute resists the air prevents him falling faster.

How gravity behaves
The Earth has a greater mass than everything upon it, so it tends to pull things on its surface down toward the centre of the earth. We call the Earth's pull gravity. It is gravity that keeps air, oceans and other objects on the Earth's surface.

Gravity pulls harder on objects with a large mass than on objects with a small mass. For instance, it pulls on a car harder than on a bicycle, and on a truck harder than on a car. When we weigh an object we are measuring the strength with which the Earth is pulling it. But weight is not the same as mass. An astronaut's mass is the same on Earth as it is on the Moon. But the Moon's pull is weaker than the Earth's so the astronaut weighs more down here on Earth than he would up on the Moon.

Although the Moon is smaller than the Earth, the Moon's own pull is strong enough to lift the sea toward it. The Moon's gravitation helps produce the high tides that sweep around the surface of the Earth's oceans.

The force of gravity depends on distance as well as mass. The greater the distance, the weaker the Earth's pulling power becomes. If the Moon's orbit was much closer to the Earth, the Earth might pull it down until it crashed, as many of the artificial satellites have done.

Space, time and light
Early this century, the German-born scientist Albert Einstein added exciting new ideas about gravitation. He showed that gravitation could affect how we measure space and time. He also showed that gravitation can bend light. This happens when the Sun passes almost in front of distant stars. The Sun's gravitation pulls their light into new paths, so making it look as if the stars have moved to new positions in the sky.

In space there is no force of gravity so astronauts just float like this. In fact these men are in a blacked-out plane that has been sent into a curving dive. They seem weightless because they are falling at the same rate as the plane around them.

CENTRIFUGAL FORCE

Hold one end of a piece of string, with a ball tied to the other end. Whirl the ball fast around your head and you feel a force pulling you off balance. This is because the ball tends to travel in a straight path, but if you force it in a curved path, as when whirling it around your head, the ball exerts an equal force against you as it tries to fly off. The force you have discovered is often called *centrifugal force.*

◀ A spinning tray whirls heavy golf balls from the middle to the rim. Lighter balls (shown black and red) move only later. A centrifuge separates light and heavy substances in this way.

▼ Chairs are flung outwards instead of hanging down as they are whirled around by a spinning chair-o-plane. Chair-o-planes are centrifuges.

Inventors have discovered several ways of using centrifugal force. Take spin driers, for instance. Maybe you have watched clothes in a spin drier. As the motor starts, they rise and go to the sides. There they stick to the drum as it spins around. When the drum stops spinning the clothes drop down again.

How centrifuges work

Machines that use centrifugal force in this way are known as centrifuges. You can get an idea of how they work by simply pouring a mixture of oil and water in a glass. After a while, the oil floats on the water, so that each liquid forms a layer. This is because oil is bulk-for-bulk lighter – less dense – than water. The pull of the earth's *gravity* makes the denser liquid sink below the other. What happens in a centrifuge is similar but faster. A centrifuge throws dense liquids to the sides more strongly than less dense liquids, but the force is far greater than that of earth's gravity. So separation of the liquids happens very quickly.

What centrifuges do

People have used simple centrifuges for hundreds of years to separate oil from water. Special modern centrifuges serve many other purposes. For instance, some separate cream from milk. Others remove the red and white blood cells from blood to leave a fluid called plasma. Plasma is often used in hospitals for blood transfusions, when a patient is given more blood. Special centrifuges can remove bacteria and dust particles from liquids.

Centrifuges have even played a part in space research. Before the first astronauts left earth they were put in special centrifuges and whirled around at high speed. This produced a gravitational pull upon their bodies many times greater than that of normal gravity. The pulling force was like that exerted on a person in a rocket speeding into space. These centrifuge experiments showed that an astronaut could best survive such forces by lying on a padded couch.

▼ Pilots carrying out these spectacular aerobatics are subject to the same centrifugal forces as clothes in a spin dryer.

COMPASSES AND GYROSCOPES

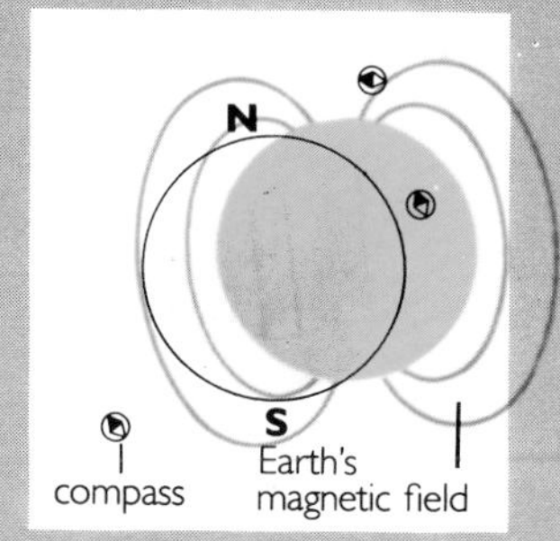

▲ The Earth's magnetic field makes compass needles dip near the north pole (N) or south pole (S). This dip could stop a needle turning freely, so it is weighted to keep it level.

Early sailors steered by using the Sun, stars or coastal landmarks as guides. But these were useless for ships sailing out of sight of land or in cloudy weather. Few sailors dared undertake such voyages before the compass was invented. The compass is an instrument that shows direction. The simplest compass is a magnetic needle free to swing from side to side. Such needles always roughly point from north to south. This is because the Earth itself behaves like a gigantic magnet, with two ends: the magnetic north and south poles. The Earth's magnetic north pole attracts one end of a compass needle, and the south pole attracts the other.

Early compasses

Early mariners knew nothing of the force of *magnetism* that makes a compass work. But the ancient Greeks discovered that a kind of iron ore attracted steel or iron. According to legend they named such pieces magnets after Magnesia, the city near where they were found.

By AD 1000 several peoples were making crude magnetic compasses. These helped Chinese and Italian navigators to steer when they were out of sight of land. The Vikings, too, may have used compasses on their voyages across the North Atlantic to North America.

An early compass was just a bit of magnetic iron fixed to a piece of cork, straw or wood floating in a bowl of water. But by the twelfth century mariners were using compasses with dials marked off into 24 or 32 points, equally spaced around the edges. They gave seamen a more accurate way of measuring direction than they had had before.

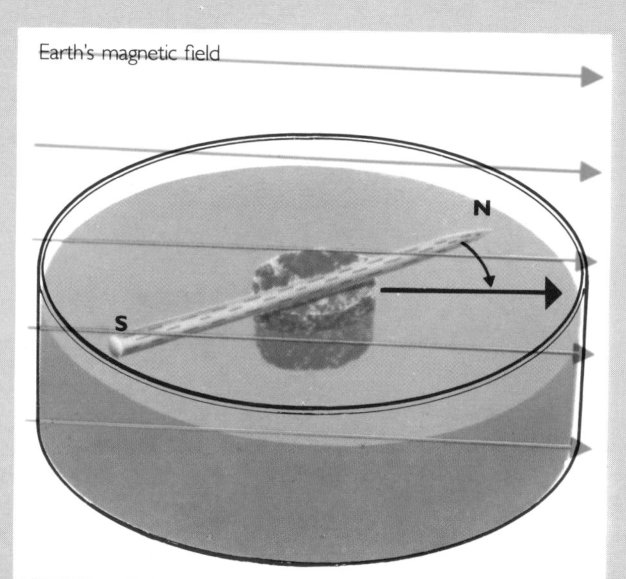

Compass points

The main compass points are north, east, south and west. These are the 'cardinal points'. Between them come the intercardinal points. For example, the intercardinal point half way between north and east is north-east. The point half way between north-east and north is north-north-east. The names of points become more clumsy the more you subdivide them. So people started naming points as degrees. There are 360 degrees in a circle such as a compass dial. Each quarter circle represents 90 degrees (shown as 90°). Measuring clockwise from 0° (North) you can call North-east 45° East, or N 45° for short. You can even drop names altogether and give points as numbers only.

Different types of compass

Magnetic compasses all work on the same principle. But there are different kinds. Scouts and explorers use a hand-held land compass. This is a magnetized needle carrying a round dial and mounted on a pivot in a case. The marine compass is more complicated, for it must stay horizontal when the ship rolls in a rough sea. The dial floats in liquid in a glass bowl. The liquid is often alcohol, which does not freeze even in the coldest weather. Aircraft compasses are different again. Instead of a swinging needle or a floating dial, they have an upright cylinder in an oil bath. The pilot or navigator can read the markings on the cylinder through a transparent panel. Ship and aircraft compasses are shielded from the effects of nearby electrical and electronic instruments, for these can make them give false readings.

◀ You do not need complicated equipment to make a magnetic compass. Rest a magnetized steel needle on a cork, float the cork in a dish of water and you have a compass!

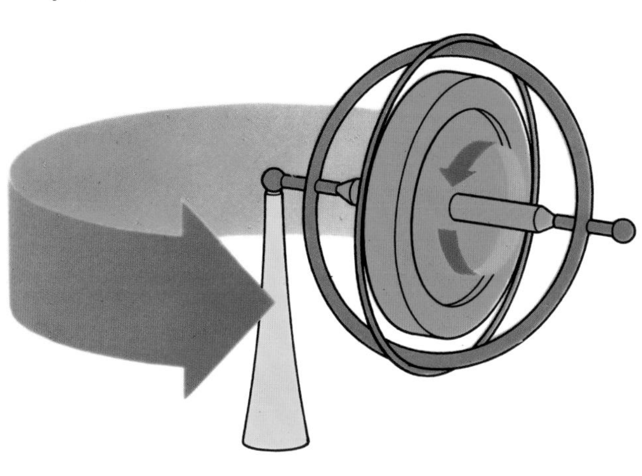

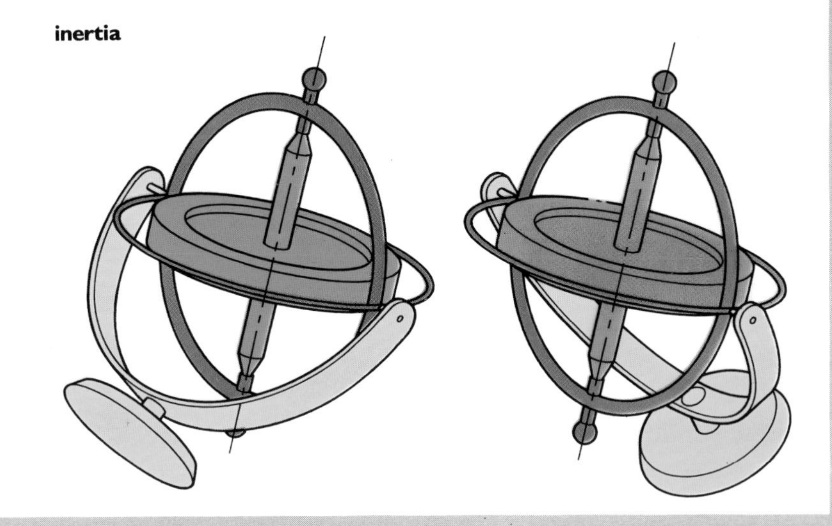

▲ Drawings show how a spinning gyroscope behaves.
Above left: The wheel or rotor (red) in guard rings (brown) spins on its axle as the small arrow shows. Because it spins it precesses or moves as shown by the brown arrow. It turns about its support but does not fall.
Above: These two diagrams show that a spinning gyroscope resists being turned when the axle is supported from both sides. Gyrocompasses use this resistance called inertia to keep them pointing to true north.

What is a gyroscope?

Gyroscopes are wheels that spin inside a movable frame. A gyroscope seems able to defy the force of gravity.

If you could point one end of the axle of a gyroscope at the Sun and keep its axle spinning fast, the axle end would seem to follow the Sun as it moves across the sky. In fact, it is the gyroscope that keeps its position while the Earth is moving under it. In 1852, the French physicist Jean Foucault used a gyroscope like this to show that the Earth turns on its axis. Foucault named the gyroscope from two Greek words for 'showing turning'.

Inertia and precession

The ability of a gyroscope's axis to keep pointing in the same direction is called gyroscopic inertia. The other unusual way in which a gyroscope behaves is called precession. This is a tendency to move at right angles to a force acting on the gyroscope. When a gyroscope spins on an upright axis, gravity pulls the gyroscope downward, but as its wheel slows down the gyroscope reacts to gravity by moving sideways like a slowly wobbling top.

The gyrocompass

Scientists use the gyroscope's unique behaviour in gyrocompasses. These do not depend on magnetism. In a gyrocompass the axle is set to point to true north at the start of a journey. Inertia keeps the gyrocompass pointing in the same direction. A special mechanism stops precession starting when the gyrocompass is disturbed. A typical modern gyrocompass has a gyroscope with a wheel 30cm (11¾in) across, spinning about 6,000 times a minute.

Gyrocompasses are usually more accurate than magnetic compasses. This is because gyrocompasses are unaffected by nearby magnetic metals, or by rolling and pitching movements. Gyrocompasses form a vital part of the navigation system in most modern ships and planes.

▲ This aircraft instrument panel includes an artificial horizon (top row centre). It is controlled by a gyroscope and shows the angle at which the plane is tilted. The dial below is a gyrocompass.

HYDROELECTRICITY

Hold a toy windmill under a tap. Falling tapwater turns the windmill's blades. The force of water flowing downhill in a river is far greater than the force of water from a tap. People had begun to put that force to work 2,000 years ago. Romans used moving water to turn the blades of watermills. These mills ground grains of wheat into flour.

By the 1880s, engineers were also using water power to generate electricity. We call this hydroelectricity from the word 'electricity' and the Greek word meaning 'water'. Today, powerful hydroelectric power stations provide some countries with much of their electric current.

A hydroelectric power station works like this: moving water spins the great blades of a wheel called an hydraulic *turbine*. The spinning turbine turns magnets near fixed coils of wire, or coils of wire near fixed magnets, so producing a powerful electric current in the wires. That current can be carried overland through other wires to bring electric current to a city.

Niagara Falls

Only certain rivers have a flow of water strong enough to operate a hydroelectric power station. The Niagara is one such river. At the Niagara Falls, between the United States and Canada, the river suddenly plunges down a cliff 64m (193ft) high. This drop gives the water great *kinetic energy* – the energy of motion. Below the falls part of that energy goes to spin the turbine blades of the Niagara Power Plant, one of the largest hydroelectric power plants anywhere. Whole cities grew up nearby to make use of its power supply.

Artificial waterfalls

Unfortunately the world does not have many waterfalls as big as the Niagara Falls. But engineers can make artificial falls by damming rivers. A dam is a strong wall that blocks a river's flow downhill toward the sea. River water collects behind the dam and rises to form a long, deep lake.

Raising the level of the water increases its potential ('stored up') energy. By letting some water escape over the dam engineers produce a man-made waterfall with enough kinetic energy to spin the turbines of a power plant. At night, when this produces more electricity than people need, engineers can use some of the

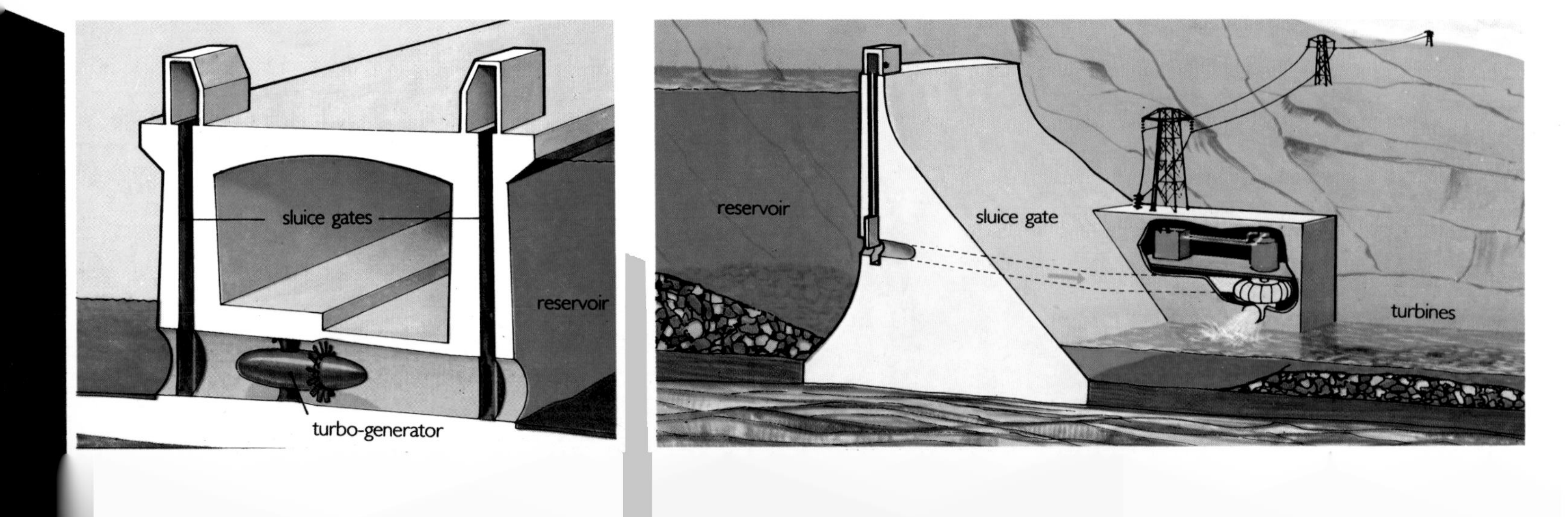

▼ A section through the Rance Barrage. The rising tide flows upstream past turbo-generators and fills the reservoir, the river above the barrage (or dam). As the tide falls, water flows out past turbo-generators in the opposite direction.

▼ This section across a dam and powerhouse shows how water produces electricity. Lifting the sluice gate lets water from the reservoir flow at high pressure along a tunnel in the dam. The water pours through the powerhouse to the river below. Turbines in the powerhouse generate electricity and cables carry it to distant cities.

Three types of turbine are used for three types of hydroelectric power plant.

◀ The Kaplan turbine works best under a low pressure head of water. It is also useful if the flow of water varies.

▲ Francis turbines work most efficiently under water that has fallen 10–100m (30–350ft).

▲ Pelton turbines work best where water has fallen more than 100m (350ft). Water jets spurt into bowl-shaped vanes or paddles.

electricity to pump water back up to the top of the dam.

Water falls farther down some dams than others. In Austria pipes carry water from one dam 1770m (5,800ft) down a cliff. That is a far greater drop than Niagara Falls.

Three types of turbine

The farther water falls to reach a turbine, the greater the water pressure. High pressure water hits turbine blades with more force than low-pressure water. Engineers build different kinds of turbine to use different kinds of water pressure. Pelton wheels (impulse turbines) take high-speed water. In a Pelton wheel, water jets strike cup-shaped paddles fixed around a spinning shaft. Pelton wheels work best in mountainous countries like Norway and Switzerland, where many lakes store water high above power stations.

Francis reaction turbines use water at medium pressure. Engineers design these turbines so that water hits all their many blades at once, and escapes through the middle of the wheel.

Kaplan turbines use low-pressure water. A Kaplan turbine looks like a ship's propeller. Its few blades lie under water. People can alter the blades' angle or 'pitch' while the turbine runs, to get the best out of changes in water pressure. Kaplan turbines work well with large amounts of low-pressure water.

Hydroelectricity has advantages over electricity produced by burning coal and oil. Hydroelectric power stations need no such fuel, so they do not poison air with smoke. In time, we shall use up all the world's coal and oil, but hydroelectricity will still be there, for most big rivers never run dry.

X-rays behave rather like beams of light. But X-rays are invisible. And unlike light they pass through such things as flesh and metal. The marks they leave upon a photographic plate can reveal things hidden deep inside such objects as a human body or a metal bridge. Experts use X-rays to detect faults that would be otherwise hidden from our eyes.

A chance discovery

The discoverer of X-rays was a German physicist named Wilhelm Konrad Roentgen. In 1895 Roentgen found X-rays almost by accident. During some experiments, he passed an electric current through Crookes tubes, special tubes from which the air had been removed. Roentgen noticed that photographic plates nearby were growing fogged. To find why, he covered a tube with black paper. Then he switched on the current. Nearby, a screen coated with the substance barium began to glow. Roentgen believed that unknown rays produced inside the tube were passing through the paper to make this fluorescent substance give out light. He called the rays X-rays because X is a scientific symbol for anything unknown.

▼ Diagrams show two types of X-ray tube. Roentgen used the simple Crookes tube when he discovered X-rays. The more powerful Coolidge tube led to the modern rotating anode X-ray tube. In these tubes, particles called electrons jump from a metal cathode to a metal anode. Hitting this turns some of the electrons' energy of movement into X-rays.

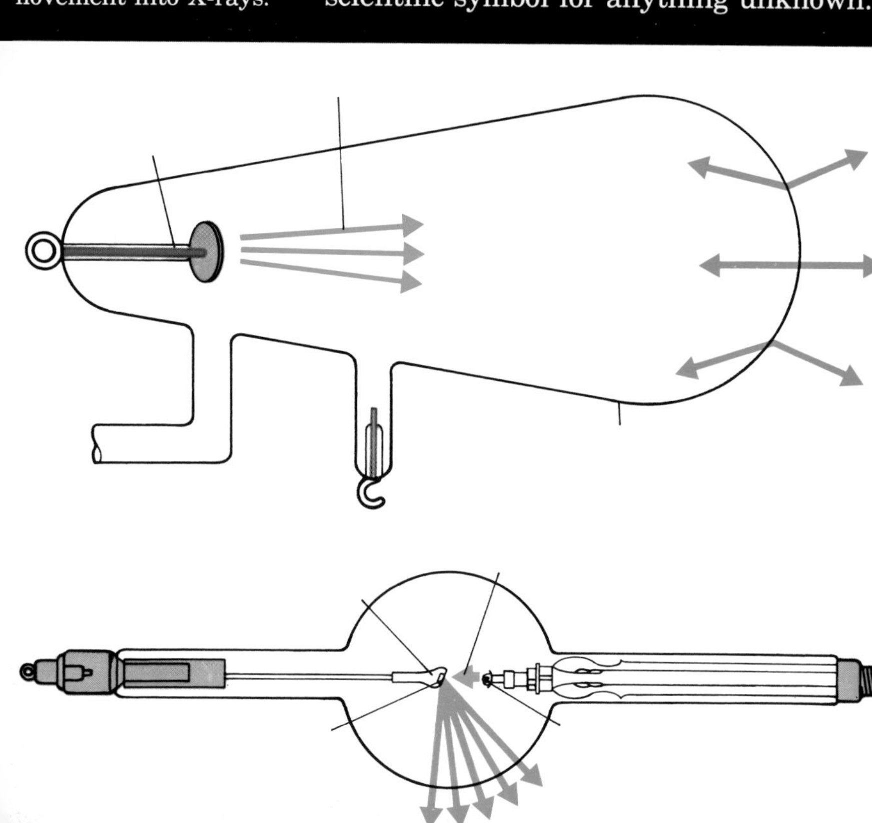

What are X-rays?

We now know that X-rays are *electromagnetic waves*, like light and radio waves. All travel at the speed of light – 300,000km (186,000 miles) per second. But the *wavelength* of an X-ray is one hundredth the wavelength of the light rays you can see. The shorter a wavelength the greater its energy. So X-rays have much more energy than light waves. This is why X-rays can pass through materials that do not let light rays through.

X-rays do not occur only on earth. For instance, astronomers have found that X-rays reach the Earth from outer space. The mysterious far-off objects known as quasars give out (emit) huge amounts of X-ray energy.

Using X-rays

With new understanding of X-rays have come new ways of using them. Airports now X-ray passengers and baggage. The X-rays will show up hidden bombs or guns. X-rays can also show art historians if a picture has been painted on an older one. X-rays can even show up loose bolts left carelessly inside an aircraft part, or cracks inside a metal structure which might lead to it collapsing.

But X-rays are used most in medicine. Hospitals are equipped with special X-ray machines. These machines photograph the insides of patients' bodies. Perhaps one patient has a broken arm or leg. The limb is put in front of the X-ray machine and a piece of photographic film is placed behind the limb. Then the X-ray machine is turned on for just a moment. X-rays pass straight through the limb's soft skin and flesh. They hit the film and show up as dark areas. But the X-rays pass less readily through hard bones. These slow down the rays and make much lighter areas on the film. So by looking at the film a doctor can see just where the bone is broken.

X-rays are so powerful that doctors can even use them to kill cancer cells inside the body. But X-rays can also harm the nearby healthy cells, so they must be used with great care.

▼ Luggage passes through an X-ray machine as part of a security check at an airport. The X-rays will give a picture of the contents of the case on a small screen.

► Dental X-ray picture of the mouth of a young adult taken from the front. The teeth are very healthy – there are no cavities or fillings. The roots of the teeth in the lower jaw show particularly clearly.

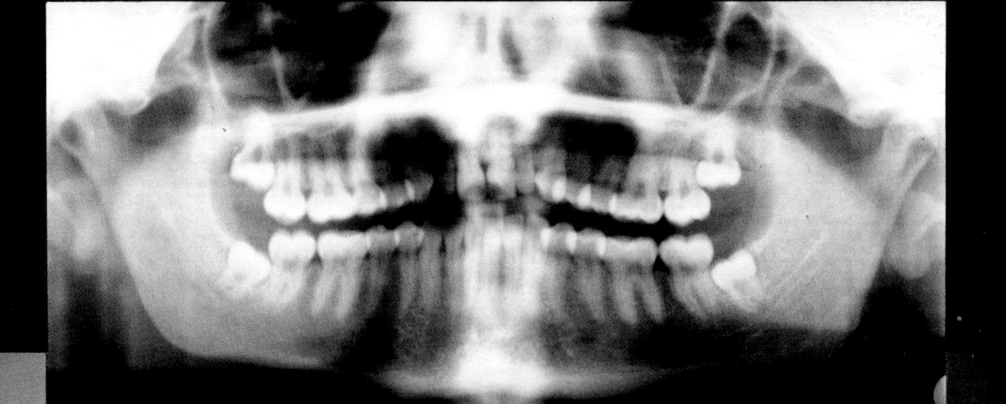

AERODYNAMICS

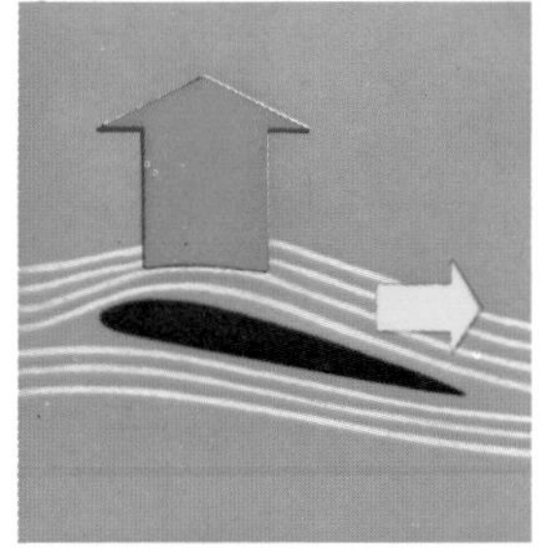

▲ When an aerofoil is at the best angle, lift (red arrow) is greatest and drag (yellow arrow) is least.

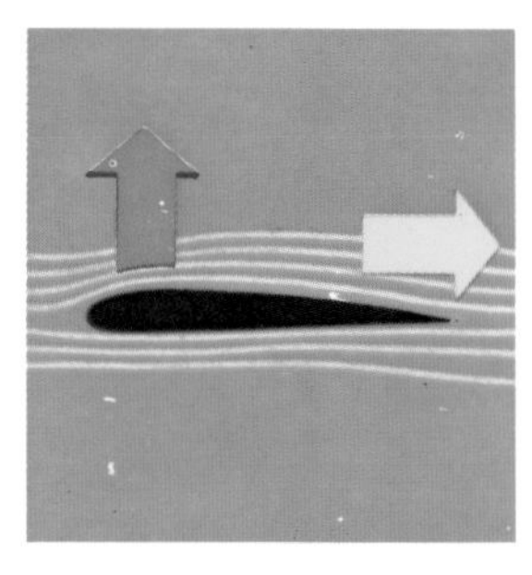

▲ At a smaller angle, lift is less and drag is greater. The best angle for lift varies with the speed.

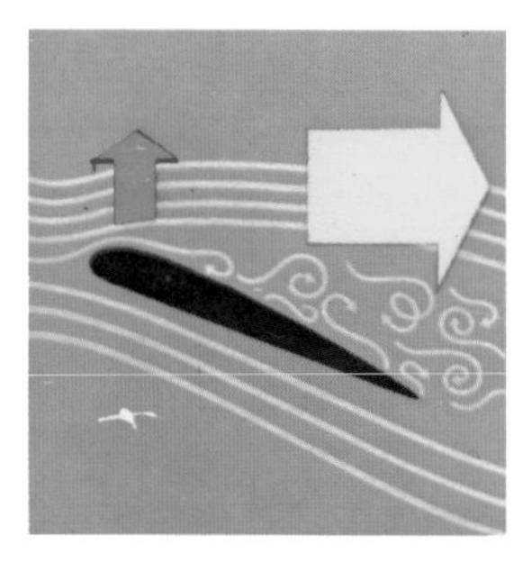

▲ An aerofoil that meets air at too great an angle breaks up the flow of air behind (pale lines). This increases drag and cuts down lift so much that the aircraft 'stalls' and falls. At low speeds it needs only a very small angle to make the aircraft stall.

Aerodynamics is the science that explains what happens when gases move past objects or objects move through gases. It explains such things as what keeps an aircraft airborne, how fast a yacht can sail, and how winds affect a bridge, an office block or a group of skyscrapers.

Discoveries in aerodynamics have made it possible to build planes that really fly, and bridges that the fiercest winds cannot blow down.

Newton and Bernoulli

It is quite easy to observe something of the forces that moving air exerts. Breezes blow leaves about. Hurricanes can smash buildings. Early inventors even put the wind to work by making windmills and sailing ships. People had been doing this for many centuries before the scientific study of mechanics revealed new ways of harnessing the power of air.

In the late 1600s the English scientist Sir Isaac Newton studied the forces that act between a fluid such as air and an object (say a house or boat). Newton noticed that the forces had the same effects whether the object moved through the fluid, or the fluid moved past the object. Later, the eighteenth-century Swiss mathematician Daniel Bernoulli made a great discovery. Bernoulli studied moving liquids in tubes. (Liquids and gases both behave similarly.) He made a tube with a narrow 'waist' and filled the tube with flowing liquid. Bernoulli found that where the liquid passed through the narrow waist it speeded up, but the pressure it exerted in all directions fell.

Bernoulli had discovered what we call Bernoulli's Principle: the greater the speed of a flowing fluid or gas, the lower its pressure.

How a plane's wings work

Inventors later used Bernoulli's Principle to produce planes that stayed up in the air. They shaped aircraft wings as aerofoils. An aerofoil is fairly flat beneath but strongly curved above. So air that flows over the wing must travel farther and faster than air that flows underneath. This means that air pressure

just above the wing is lower than air pressure just beneath (or even well above the wing). So the wing feels an upward force called lift. If lift is stronger than the downward pull produced by the plane's weight, the plane stays airborne.

Drag and streamlining

The faster the plane flies, the greater the lift. But air also produces a backward resisting force called drag. This force increases with the plane's speed.

Designers try to shape planes to produce as much lift and as little drag as possible. They do this largely by giving planes smooth, curved bodies. This is

▲ This end-on view shows aerodynamic testing of a model of the Concorde supersonic airliner, placed in a tank of oil. Oil imitates the way air would behave when stirred up by the high-speed plane in flight.

◀ Models of these new office buildings were tested in a wind-tunnel. The smoke blown through the tunnel showed that the buildings' shapes caused strong gusts of wind between the buildings. The architects had to change their design and roof the space over to stop the gusts of wind.

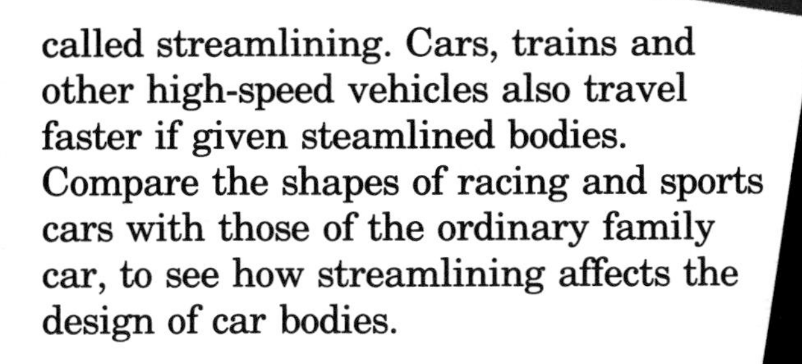

called streamlining. Cars, trains and other high-speed vehicles also travel faster if given steamlined bodies. Compare the shapes of racing and sports cars with those of the ordinary family car, to see how streamlining affects the design of car bodies.

ROCKETS

By 1950, there were jet planes fast enough to carry people around the world in just one day. But no one had ever left the Earth and travelled out through space to the Moon or planets. There were two reasons: one was the downward tug of gravity. The other reason was the lack of air in space. To overcome the pull of gravity you must speed upward at 40,000kph (25,000mph). No machine could go that fast in 1950. Anyway planes and other vehicles were powered by engines that burnt fuel in oxygen obtained from air. There *is* no air in empty space.

How rockets work

The invention that made space flight possible was the rocket. Rockets do not need to suck in air for oxygen. They contain their own oxidants – oxygen-rich substances for burning fuel. Also, a rocket travels faster through empty space than through the air, which slows it down.

How rockets work was first explained three centuries ago. The English scientist

◀ The Saturn V three-stage launcher took the first men to the Moon. Each stage is powered by rocket engines. Here, the five huge F-1 first stage engines, fuelled by oxygen and paraffin, fire at the take-off.

▼ Engineers watch instruments that tell them if a rocket system is behaving properly. Such instruments make it possible for experts here on earth to launch a rocket and steer it far through space.

Sir Isaac Newton said that every action has an opposite and equal reaction. For example, a bullet fired from a gun barrel makes the gun kick backward. Jumping ashore from a small boat thrusts the boat offshore. So, too, with rockets. Burning fuel inside a rocket gives off hot gas. Heat makes the gas expand, so it escapes quickly from a hole at the back of the rocket. The backward movement of this jet of gas is an action that makes a rocket travel forward by reaction.

◀ A German V2 rocket designed for use against the British Isles in World War 2. It is being raised from its trailer to the vertical firing position.

The story of the rocket

People were making rockets long before they knew how rockets worked. The first rockets used gunpowder. Seven centuries ago Chinese troops were firing explosive rockets at their enemies. Later, Indian, Arab and European armies developed rocket weapons.

By 1900 rockets were still weak and difficult to control. But in 1883 the Russian schoolteacher Konstantin Tsiolkovsky suggested that a powerful rocket could be used for travel in space. Tsiolkovsky realized that liquid fuel could make a rocket more powerful and easier to control than the solid fuel that had been used in rockets up till then.

In 1926 the American Robert H. Goddard launched a tiny liquid-fuelled rocket. By 1942 Germany had the first powerful long-range rockets. These V2s stood nearly 15m (50ft) high and could fly 200km (125 miles) before exploding on the ground. The V2 was a war weapon. But American rocket researchers later used V2s to help them develop much larger and more powerful rockets. Meanwhile, the Soviet Union began to build big rockets of its own.

Multi-stage rockets

The Soviet Union and the United States both developed space vehicles which were shot up into the sky by sets of rockets mounted one above the other. Each of these multi-stage rockets has its own fuel tanks and engines. Each rocket's engines fire in turn. When the bottom rocket's fuel is finished the second rocket's engine fires. Meanwhile the bottom rocket falls back down to Earth. And so on. This system thrusts the small top rocket and its payload far higher and faster than it would go if it had taken off alone. Multi-stage rockets have helped men reach the Moon.

The American Space Shuttle is a rocket plane. A huge Saturn V rocket carries the shuttle far up into the sky. Then the shuttle's engines fire and take it into orbit around the Earth. Later, the pilot-craft glides back down again. Unlike most space rockets, this rocket plane can make many space flights without becoming lost or damaged.

▼ The American Space Shuttle returns to Earth after a successful flight. Although launched into orbit by a rocket that is destroyed in the process, the Space Shuttle can be used many times.

RADAR

▲ No busy modern international airport could function without radar. This large radar antenna is just one part of the air traffic control system keeping track of the positions of all the aircraft taking off and coming in to land.

If you shout inside an empty hall you hear an echo. This echo is the sound of your own voice being bounced back from the walls. A flying bat makes high-pitched squeaks and listens to the echoes that bounce back off solid objects. The nearer the object the sooner the echo returns, so the bat knows how far away objects are. Echoes help bats to dodge trees or buildings and to catch flying insects, even on the darkest nights.

Radio echoes

Radar is a man-made navigation system that depends on echoes. Radar devices help planes to fly at night without colliding. Radar helps ships to sail in fog or darkness without the risk of hitting other ships, or rocks close to the surface of the water.

Radar uses short *radio* waves instead of sounds. Radio waves travel much farther and faster through air than sound waves do. Radio waves move as fast as light – this is about 300,000km (186,000 miles) per second. A radar set sends out short bursts of radio waves. If there is an aircraft in their path, some hit the plane and bounce back to the radar set, just like sound echoes.

A radar set automatically measures the time taken for this double journey. The set also 'knows' the speed of radio waves. It puts all this information together to show the plane's direction and distance. In fact, the word radar is short for *ra*dio *d*etection *a*nd *r*anging. 'Ranging' means measuring distance.

A radar set has two main parts: transmitter and receiver. The transmitter produces and sends out radio waves. The receiver detects returning echoes. To produce a strong echo, the set must send out waves in powerful bursts, or pulses. Also it must aim these in a narrow beam. To focus waves like this many radar sets have a big dish-shaped antenna jutting up into the air. The antenna swings back and forth or moves around and around. The antenna beams out waves like a search-light. When the antenna receives an echo from an object, this object is in the direction to which the antenna is pointing at that moment.

Radar echoes show up as bright spots on a radar screen. These tell the radar operator the distance and direction of the object that produced the echoes.

Radar development

The invention of radar depended on the work of many scientists. For instance, the German scientist Heinrich Hertz discovered radio waves in the 1880s. The Italian inventor Guglielmo Marconi produced the first radio transmitting equipment in the 1890s. By the middle 1930s, American and British scientists had made the first pulse radar systems. Soon, several other countries had radar of their own.

Radar developed fast in World War 2. Modern military radar can detect far-off enemy ships and planes. Radar also makes it easy to aim guns, bombs or rockets accurately at a target.

Radar now has many peace-time uses. Ships and aircraft use radar for navigation. Air traffic controllers rely on radar to prevent planes colliding as they land or take off at an airport. Traffic police use radar to check the speed of vehicles. Weathermen use radar to detect and follow hurricanes. Radar even helps astronomers to study meteors and planets.

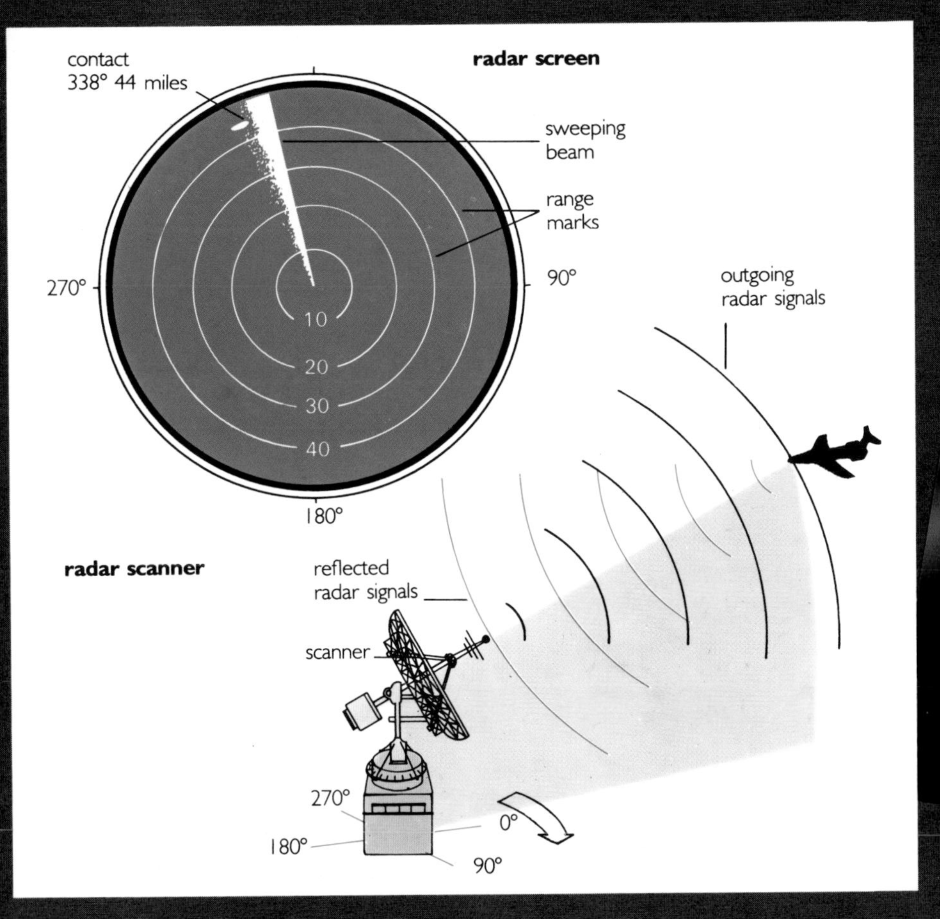

▲ When outgoing radar signals hit a target some are reflected back to the radar set (above). This machine measures the time taken for each signal's journey out and back. Time taken shows the target's distance. On the radar screen (top) a blip of light shows the target's range and angle from the observer.

▲ Radar antennae aboard an American aircraft carrier help the ship to keep in radar touch with its planes.

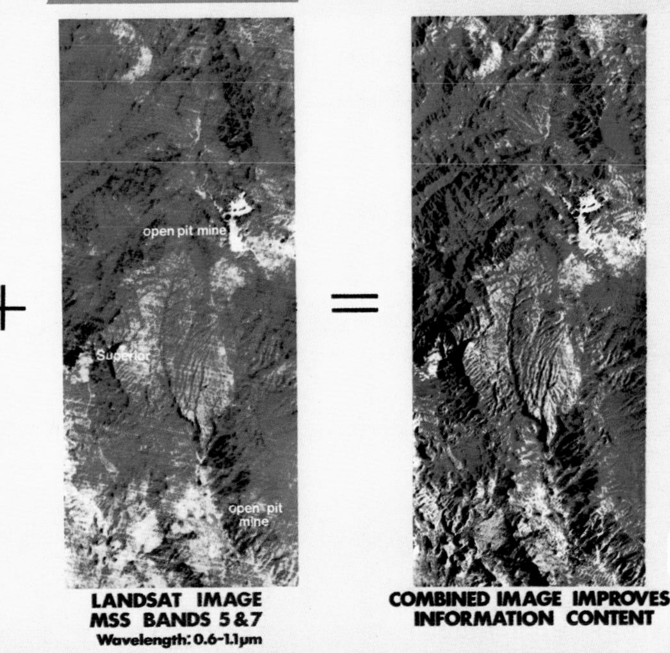

◄ These three pictures of the same site in Arizona form part of the US Geological Survey. They show very vividly how modern technology enables scientists to get an excellent overview of the Earth's surface. Forty years ago it would have been quite impossible to

NUCLEAR ENERGY

Energy is the ability to do work. Without energy no fire would burn, no living thing would grow. No vehicle would move. No star would shine.

There are many kinds of energy. Solar energy (the Sun's energy) heats and lights the Earth. Mechanical energy turns wheels. Chemical energy is stored in fuels like wood and coal. Electrical energy flows through wires into your home.

We can turn one kind of energy into another. For instance, when you light a coal fire, chemical energy stored in coal turns into heat energy. Heat can be used to produce electrical energy and *electricity* can produce heat, light, sound or mechanical energy.

This century, the world's demands for energy have risen fast; we have been using up rapidly the supplies of fuels including coal, oil, gas and wood. So scientists set out to find new sources of energy. The most amazing and immensely powerful source they found was the energy locked up in those tiny particles of matter, atoms (page 12).

Splitting atoms

Early this century, scientists realized that each atom's core, or nucleus, contained close-packed particles called protons and neutrons. They found that these particles were bound together by immensely powerful forces. Bit by bit, physicists found it was possible to overcome these forces – to split one kind of atom in a way that set free huge amounts of energy.

In the winter of 1938–39, the German scientist Otto Hahn and his colleague K Strassman showed that if neutrons bombarded *uranium* atoms, some neutrons hit the uranium nuclei and made them split in two. They called this splitting nuclear *fission*. The splitting atoms gave off neutrons and other particles. If one of these neutrons struck another atom, it had the force to split that too and set off yet more neutrons. If enough neutrons could be set off in this way, they would start a chain reaction unleashing vast quantities of energy. An Italian-born physicist, Enrico Fermi, produced the world's first controlled nuclear chain reaction in the United States in 1942.

Nuclear fission at work

In 1945, in World War 2, the United States dropped two nuclear fission bombs upon Japan. Each destroyed a city, and the first exploded with 2,000 times the force of an ordinary bomb.

Since World War 2, scientists have put nuclear energy to work in peaceful ways. In buildings known as *nuclear reactors*, scientists control chain reactions to make them give off heat. This heat turns water into steam. The steam spins the blades of turbines that in turn produce electric current. A single nuclear reactor can generate enough electric current to supply a city. Scores of nuclear reactors are now operating around the world.

Nuclear fusion

Splitting the big nucleus of a uranium atom is not the only way of getting huge amounts of energy from atoms. Forcing small atomic nuclei to fuse together helps to release energy in even larger quantities. In 1948, American scientists used uranium fission to fuse hydrogen atoms, releasing extra energy to split still more uranium. Hydrogen bombs that work like this are many hundred times more damaging than were the first atomic bombs. But by the 1980s scientists were still seeking ways to use this energy for peaceful purposes. They faced many problems, and the first nuclear *fusion* reactor still seems a long way off.

▼ Niels Bohr (1885–1962) was a Danish scientist who discovered much about how atoms are made and split to yield huge amounts of energy. This diagram shows his idea of what happens when a neutron (black dot) hits a uranium nucleus (red). The nucleus splits in two like drops of liquid, to produce two nuclei of elements that are not uranium. Meanwhile more neutrons escape and might set off reactions in more uranium atoms.

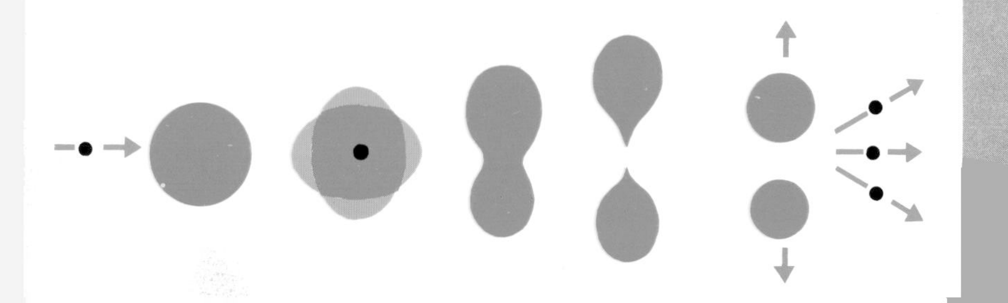

◀ A nuclear scientist checking machinery in a nuclear power station in Philadelphia, USA.

▼ Inside a nuclear power station, showing where the uranium piles are placed.

▼ The nuclear power station at Dounreay in Scotland was one of the first of the fast breeder reactors.

ELECTRONICS

► This integrated circuit has 50 parts built into a silicon chip about 1mm ($\frac{1}{32}$in) square in size.

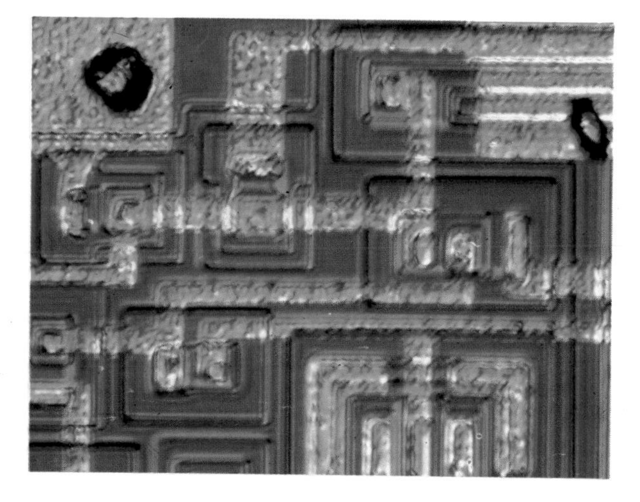

Most of us watch television and listen to radios and tape recorders. Some people work with X-ray machines, electron microscopes or radar sets. All these devices depend on tiny, carefully controlled electric currents. An electric current is a flow of negatively charged particles called electrons. *Electronics* is the science of controlling how electrons flow.

Inside an electronic device, a wire or other piece of metal emits (gives off) electrons, so it is called the emitter. A positively charged metal plate nearby attracts electrons. They leave their wire and leap a gap to reach the plate.

In the 1890s scientists began developing the first electronic devices, usually keeping them in a glass or metal tube almost emptied of air.

▼ The electron tube (also known as a thermionic valve or vacuum tube) was the invention that made electronics possible.

Diodes and triodes

The simplest electron tubes are called *diodes* (*di* means two) because they have just two main parts: an emitter and a plate. In 1904 a British scientist, John Fleming, built a diode tube able to detect radio signals. Diodes proved immensely useful because they could change alternating electric currents – the kind supplied by power stations – into direct current, the kind that radios and televisions use.

In 1907 the American inventor, Lee de Forest, produced a second great invention, called a *triode* (*tri* means three). This tube has three main parts: an emitter, a plate and a grid between the other two. A positive electric charge applied to the grid draws many extra electrons from the emitter, and sends a strong electric current through the tube. Triodes can strengthen the weak signals received by radio and television sets. They made modern radio and television broadcasts possible.

Transistors and integrated circuits

In 1947 American scientists led by William Shockley produced the first *transistor*. Transistors use small pieces of substances called *semiconductors*. Semiconductors can be arranged to act in the same way as electron tubes, to amplify, or strengthen, electric signals. But transistors are much lighter, smaller, and longer-lasting than glass *electron tubes*.

Today, whole complicated electronic pathways called *integrated circuits* can be built into or on a chip smaller than your little fingernail. Such chips are often made of the semiconductor substance silicon. Integrated circuits have helped electronics experts to build even smaller yet more powerful computers.

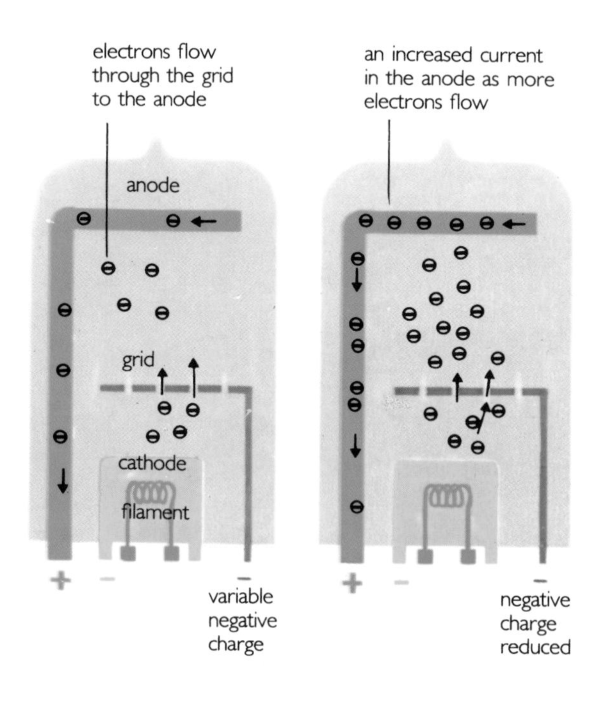

▲ In a triode, electrons flow from cathode (red) to anode (green). The flow is controlled by small changes in voltage (electrical pressure) applied to the grid (dark blue). Triodes can boost television and radio signals.

▼ High aerials such as this beam out electromagnetic signals, which are magnified by electron tubes or transistors in our radio and television sets.

▲ Integrated circuits are so tiny that thousands fit into the thimble shown beside this pencil.

▼ Electronics is a fast developing science. Although barely 30 years old, the wiring and large valves of this electronic circuit seem very clumsy compared with modern integrated circuits (**above left**)

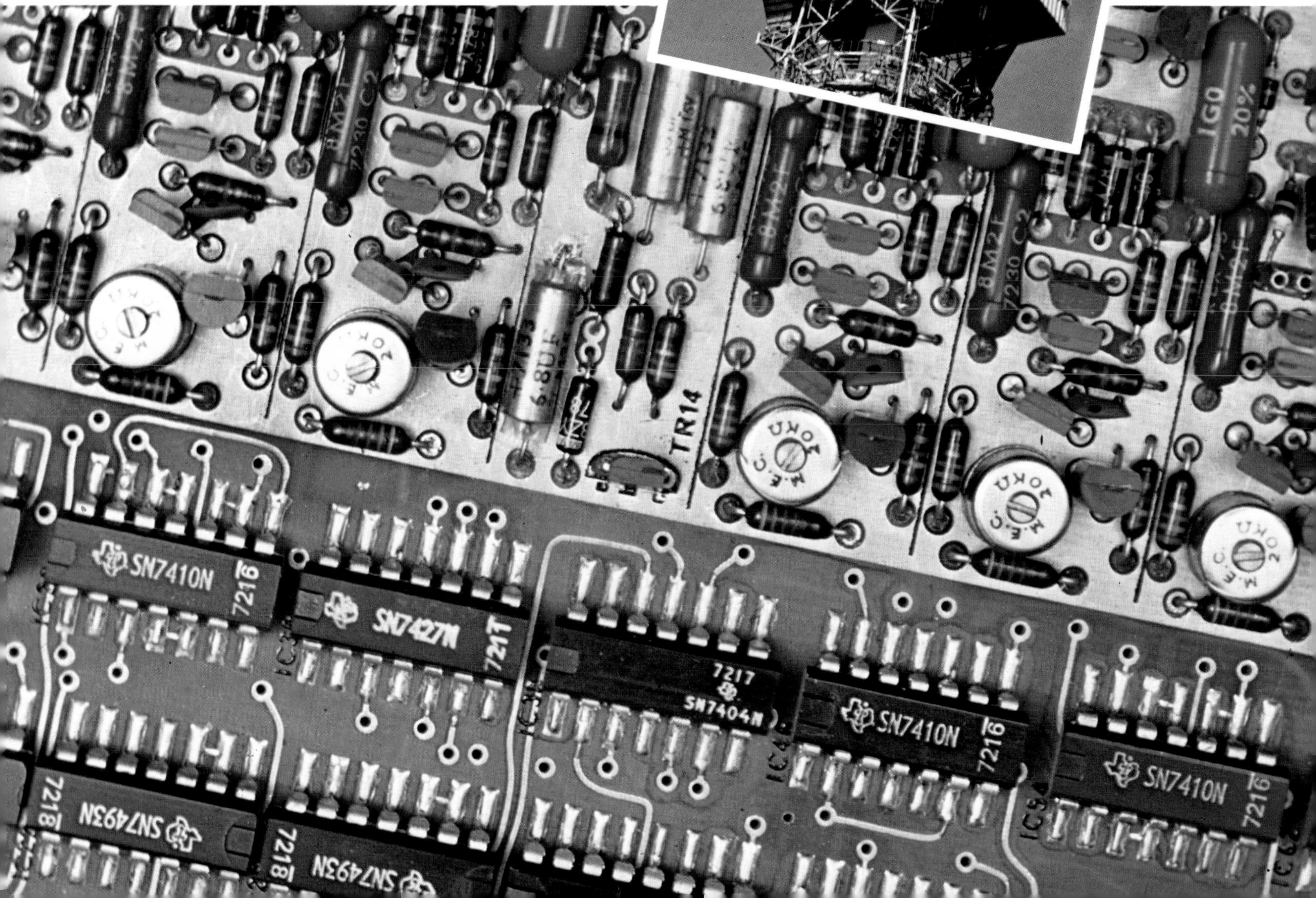

LASERS

The word 'laser' is short for '*l*ight *a*mplification by *s*timulated *e*mission of *r*adiation'. Lasers are devices that strengthen, or amplify, light energy. A high power laser could burn a hole through a diamond, the hardest substance known.

Laser light

The light produced by lasers differs from the light from an electric bulb or from the Sun. These beam out light in all directions. Also their light is made up of many colours, each produced by light of a different wavelength. A laser sends out a narrow beam of light in only one direction. A laser beam pointed at the Moon makes a disc of light on the Moon's surface only 3km (1¾ miles) across. Also laser light tends to go out at one wavelength, so it has one colour. Laser light is a powerfully concentrated form of energy.

▼ Surgeons using a laser to treat skin cancer. The cancerous tissue absorbs the laser's light and is destroyed. Normal skin is hardly affected at all by the laser.

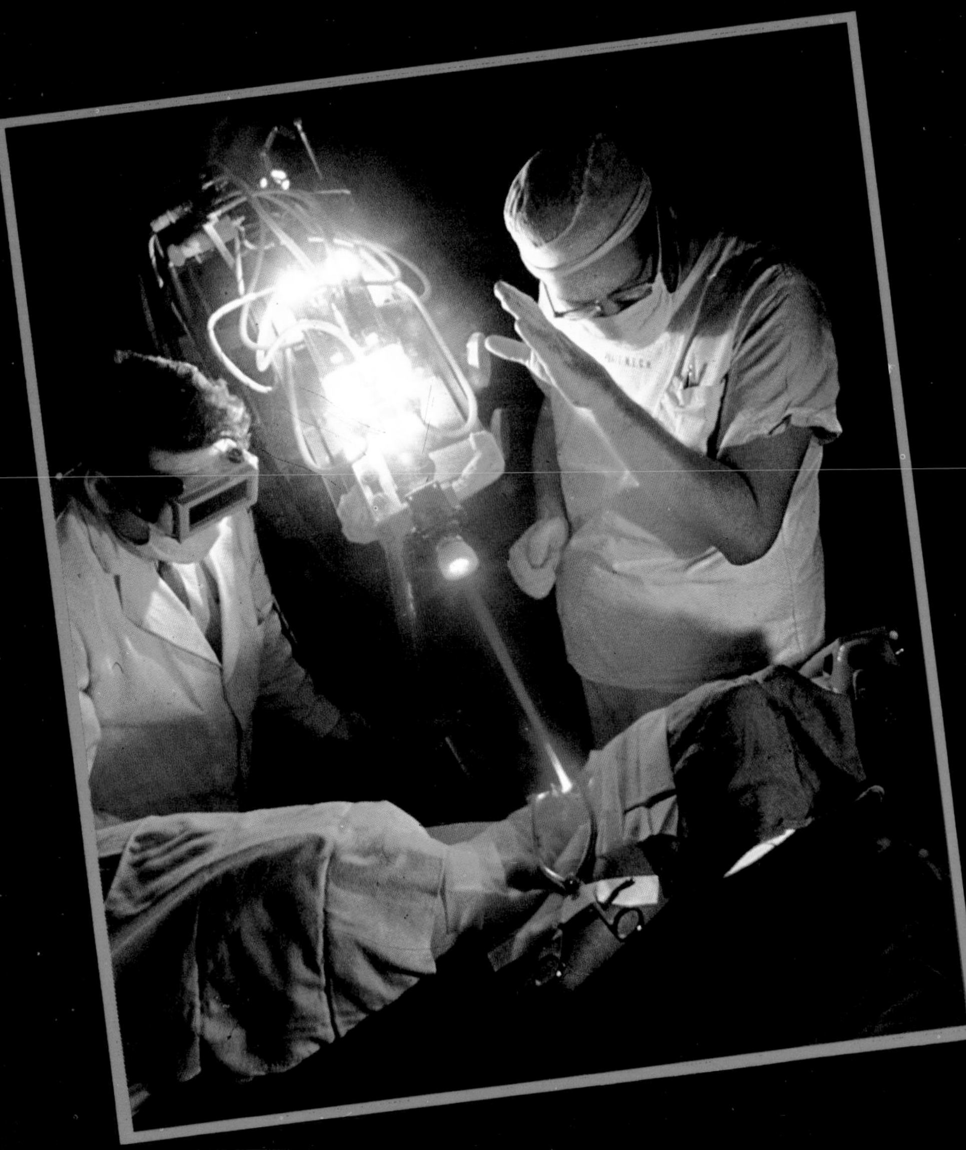

How lasers work

There are two main kinds of laser: solid and gas. Many solid lasers contain a rod-shaped ruby crystal the size of a pencil. One end is silver coated to reflect all light reaching it from inside the crystal. The other end is partly silver coated and reflects some light but lets the rest escape. A flash tube is coiled around the ruby crystal. The tube sends a dazzling flash of light through the crystal. This flash gives extra energy to atoms in the crystal. We say such atoms have become excited. Excited atoms in turn excite yet other atoms. All give off their extra energy as light. As it is reflected to and fro inside the crystal, the light hits more and more excited atoms, so making the light grow stronger. Suddenly this build-up of extra energy sets off a powerful pulse of light. This pulse runs through the crystal and streams out from the partly silvered end as a narrow beam.

Gas lasers work in a similar way, but use a tube of gas instead of a crystal rod to amplify, or strengthen, light, and give a steady beam instead of pulses.

The laser's story

Two American scientists, Arthur Schawlow and Charles Townes, first came up with the idea of the laser in 1958. The first working ruby laser was made in 1960. The following year, 1961, a laser was produced that gave off a steady beam of light.

Today, doctors use laser beams to repair certain kinds of damage to the human eye. Craftsmen use laser beams to melt and weld together tiny bits of metal. Engineers can produce a single beam to carry many telephone or television signals. Astronomers have even measured the exact distance between the Moon and Earth by bouncing laser light off mirrors on the Moon. Video discs are 'read' by laser beams.

▼ This man is working with a gas laser. The lens and prisms focus light waves onto atoms of the gas inside the laser (*left*). This excites the atoms and they boost the light into an intense and very narrow beam.

◀ Lasers can have less serious uses. These lasers are part of a Christmas display of lights in London's Oxford Street.

Holography is a photographic method of making pictures called holograms that look as real and solid as the objects that they show. Such three-dimensional, or '3-D', pictures have depth as well as length and breadth. The idea of holography has been around since about 1940. But this way of making images remained impossible until the coming of the laser.

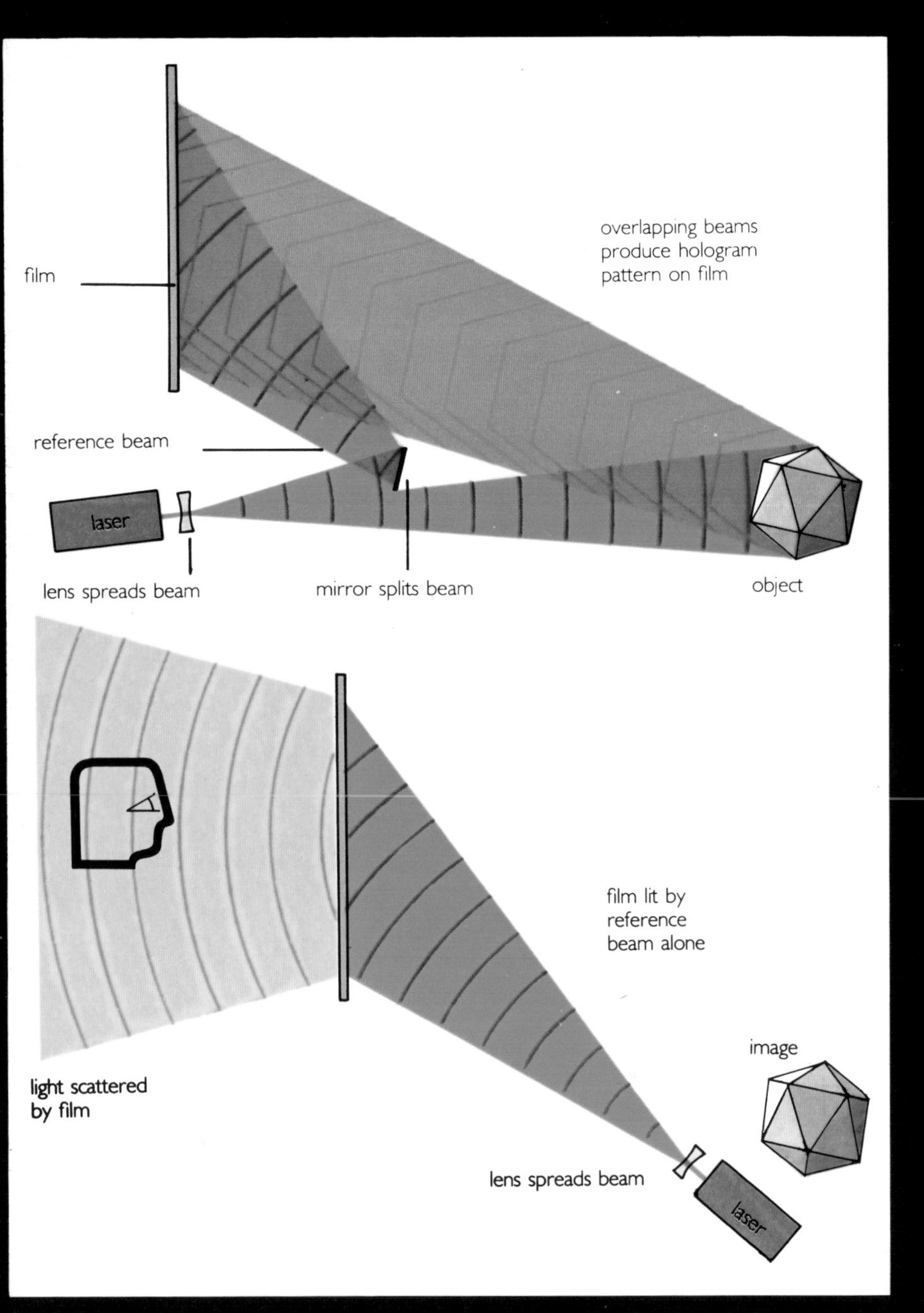

▲ Making a hologram (top). In the reference beam laser light waves are all in step; those from the object are not. The two beams make a pattern of light and dark patches on the film.
Viewing a hologram (above). Laser light passed through the developed film spreads out. The viewer sees an image of the original object.

Making a hologram

To make a hologram you aim a laser beam at the object to be holographed. Laser light waves are all the same length and keep in step with one another. This is unlike ordinary light which is made of light waves that have different lengths and travel out of step with one another.

A mirror half-way along the laser beam reflects half the beam onto an ordinary photographic film. This half of the beam is called the reference beam. The other half of the beam shines directly on the object, and some of this light is bounced back to the film. This part of the beam is the signal beam. Those waves that reach the back of the object travel farther than those that only reach the front. But waves in the reference beam always travel the same distance. So when both sets of waves meet at the film some have become out of step with the others. Where waves from the signal beam and reference beam arrive in step they reinforce each other to produce bright light. This makes a clear patch on the film. Waves arriving out of step cancel out each other and produce a dark patch on the film. The pattern of dark and clear patches records not just the object's shape but which parts are nearer than others. The developed film is called a hologram.

Viewing a hologram

If you look at a hologram in ordinary light you see only a jumble of spots and lines. But shine a laser light of the same wavelength as the first one through it and you notice something very different. The light passes only through the film's clear patches. On the film's far side the light emerges in a pattern of brightness and darkness exactly like the pattern made by the overlapping reference beam and reflected signal beam. The light that has passed through the hologram spreads out like light from the original scene. So anyone in the path of the light sees an exact replica of the actual object.

Holograms are used in computer memories and for measuring small vibrations. And holography could produce a new system of 3-D motion pictures.

◀ Holograms such as these two are little more than modern conjuring tricks – the man is real but the tap and the apples (**below**) are not. Already, however, scientists are using holograms – 3-dimensional photographs of objects – to help them in their research, and they are also used in computer memories.

Acids Chemical compounds that tend to taste sour, attack metals, and turn blue litmus paper red. Acids combine with alkalis to make salts and water.
Alkalis Chemical substances that turn red litmus paper blue and cancel out the effects of acids. They are sometimes called bases.
Annealing Slow cooling of molten glass or metal to stop it cracking. Heat treatment of metal to toughen it.
Anode The positive electrode in an electron tube or similar device.
Atom The smallest particle of matter able to take part in a chemical change, and containing electrons, protons and neutrons.
Carbohydrate A chemical compound made only of carbon, hydrogen and oxygen. Starch and sugar are carbohydrates.
Carbon An element found in coal, diamonds, carbon dioxide gas and some other substances.
Cathode The negative electrode in an electron tube or similar device. It emits electrons.
Cellulose A chemical compound that forms the cell walls of plants.
Centrifugal force An outward force that acts on an object turning in a circle around a central point.
Chromatography A way of separating the substances in mixtures.
Compound A substance made of atoms of at least two elements chemically joined together.
Copper A soft reddish metal. It was the first metal used for making metal tools.
Diode An electron tube containing two electrodes, one an anode, the other a cathode and allowing current to go in one direction only.
Electric charge An imbalance in the number of electrons or protons between electrodes or other objects. Electricity tends to flow between objects with opposite electric charges.
Electricity Energy associated with a flow of electrons or other charged particles.
Electrode An electrical conductor through which an electric current leaves or enters an electron tube or similar device. Anodes and cathodes are electrodes.
Electromagnetic wave A wave of energy produced by an electric charge. Light and radio signals travel as electromagnetic waves.
Electron Sub-atomic particle with a negative electric charge.
Electronics The study of devices such as diodes or valves where electrons pass through a semiconductor, gas or vacuum, as in computers, radios or televisions.
Electron microscope A microscope that magnifies with the help of streams of electrons instead of light rays.
Electron tube A tube controlling a flow of electrons, for instance a diode, triode or television tube.
Element A substance made only of one kind of atom.
Engine A device that changes one form of energy into another.
Fission Splitting.
Fusion Melting together.
Gears Toothed wheels as used in steering and other power-transmission systems.
Gravitation The force that attracts every particle in the Universe to every other particle.
Gravity The force of gravitation exerted by the Earth.
Hydrogen The lightest element in the Universe with the smallest atom.
Integrated circuit A tiny mass of electronic components in or on a small slice of semiconductor substance.
Iron An abundant metal element used for making many kinds of tools and structures.
Kinetic energy The energy of motion.
Lens A device that makes a beam of rays spread out or grow narrower.
Machine A device that harnesses energy.
Magnetism The attraction exerted by iron when its molecules are lined up in rows.

◀ Carving in stone of a sailing ship of a kind that traded round the Mediterranean Sea many centuries ago. The sun and the stars were the main navigational aids for sailors in those days.

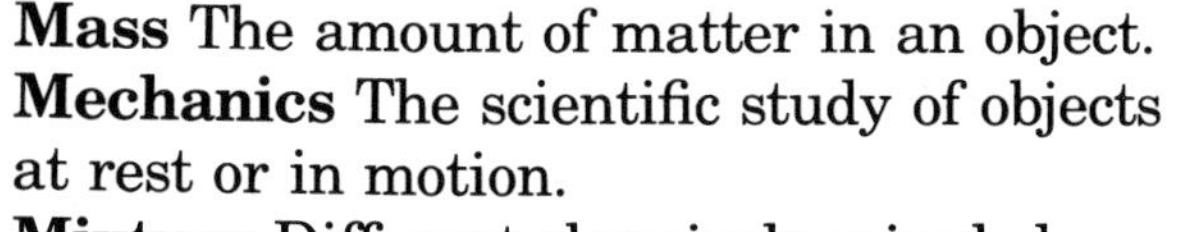

Mass The amount of matter in an object.
Mechanics The scientific study of objects at rest or in motion.
Mixture Different chemicals mingled together but not chemically joined.
Molecule The smallest possible particle of a chemical compound that can exist, consisting of two or more atoms that are chemically joined.
Motor A device that changes some other kind of energy into mechanical energy; the energy found in machines.
Neutron One kind of particle in an atom's nucleus. Neutrons have no electric charge.
Nuclear reactor A power station producing electricity from energy released by splitting the nuclei of atoms.
Nucleus, atomic The core of an atom, containing at least one proton and usually one or more neutrons.
Polymer A long-chain molecule made up of several smaller molecules occuring again and again.
Pressure A force acting on a surface.
Proton One kind of particle in an atom's nucleus. Protons have a positive electric charge.
Radio A system using electromagnetic waves to send signals long distances without wires. Radio, radar, and television all work this way.
Semiconductor Material that conducts electricity not as well as conductors such as copper, but better than insulators such as glass.
Steel A hard, tough form of iron and carbon.

▲ This is a yacht compass. Iron balls on each side of it are adjusted to correct any errors and make sure the compass points to the magnetic north pole.

Synthetic Made artificially by chemical reactions.
Technologist An expert who puts scientific knowledge to work for practical purposes.
Transistor A device using semiconductors to amplify electric signals.
Triode An electron tube containing a cathode, an anode and a grid to control the current between them.
Turbine A motor with a shaft spun by a flow of gas or liquid. Turbines linked to electric generators produce electric current.
Uranium An element with a large atomic nucleus, fairly easy to split. Splitting the nuclei of one type of uranium produces chain reactions in nuclear reactors.
Wavelength The distance between two successive wave crests or similar points, in a row of waves.

INDEX

Acknowledgements

A–Z Collection; Ron Boardman; Camera Press; Richard Cooke; Courtaulds Ltd; Daily Telegraph Colour Library; Douglas Dickens; Doulton and Co Ltd; IAL Security Systems; IBM; Archivio IGDA/Archivio B, C Bevilacqua, P Castano, Dagli Orti, Foto Miglio, Marka, F Arborio Mella, G Nimatallah, ONERA, RAI, B Richner, R Thuillier, Titus; Imperial War Museum; Kunstmuseum Lucerne; NASA; OPI; Parfitt; Pershing Price Ltd; Picturepoint; Rex Features; Science Photo Library; Shell Photographic Library; Societa Generale Semicondutton; Spectrum Colour Library; St Andrews University; Taurus Photo; Toledo Museum of Art; USIS; Vauxhall/Opel; Josiah Wedgwood and Sons Ltd; ZEFA.